Take The High Road

it's not where you begin it's how you
finish; a MUST READ for those
with disabilities and addictions

A story of hope, recovery and happiness
It doesn't matter where you start
It's where you finish

Jeffrey Claude Parker, MSW

authorHOUSE®

AuthorHouse™
1663 Liberty Drive
Bloomington, IN 47403
www.authorhouse.com
Phone: 1 (800) 839-8640

Published by AuthorHouse 09/27/2019

ISBN: 978-1-7283-2913-0 (sc)
ISBN: 978-1-7283-2911-6 (hc)
ISBN: 978-1-7283-2912-3 (e)

Library of Congress Control Number: 2019915059

Print information available on the last page.

CONTENTS

PREMISE

I used to say that I was dealt a bad hand from the start and for that reason, I did not have a chance to be successful or happy in life. I have come to find that being dealt a bad hand (so to speak) is what helped me become more resilient and tolerant of life's problems. Ultimately, it is what forced me to become desperate enough to change the way I was living my life.

Just because one has been dealt a bad hand does not mean that your life will end up in a bad way. It is not where you start, it's where you finish. Adversity made me desperate enough to reach out and use the resources available to improve my life.

I finally faced the many different problems I had been running from for many years. Avoiding problems allows them to grow and become more debilitating and overwhelming. I was surviving but not living because I was living in avoidance mode. I dealt with my problems by not dealing with them.

Alcohol was the thing that helped me to get through each day so that I could struggle more the next. Alcohol made what was bad even worse, and I reached a point where I gave up and no longer cared. I was looking for immediate relief every day and drinking was the way I did that.

Immediate gratification is a frequently used term, but gratified was not what I felt. Drowning myself in self-pity and liquor and smoking marijuana the first half of my life was not gratifying in the least. How can I be gratified when I was unconscious or numb most of the time?

This book is dedicated to my late mother, Claudette Parker, who was with me during the bad times and unlike my father, lived long enough to see the good. She was able to see the metamorphosis. She saw the radical changes her son had made, like a caterpillar to a butterfly. She was proud of her once troubled and disabled child for becoming a responsible man who is now living a normal and happy life.

The bottom line is that it doesn't matter the hand we are dealt. What does matter, are the choices we make because they all have consequences. It is about recognizing the unhealthy cycles we have created and doing what is needed to break those cycles and create new and healthy ones.

My motivation for sharing my story is to show that victory is possible regardless of the problems and challenges we encounter. The key is to face challenges and not run from them. My mission is to instill hope in those who are struggling and are in a dark place. So frequently today, the focus is our differences. At the end of this book, my wish is that the reader can see that adversity is something that we all will be confronted with, and that it is inevitable.

I have a lot of experience in group counseling in my career. Being a group facilitator has enabled me to hear many problems that clients are faced with. The most frequent response when asking them how they benefited by attending group is that they see that they are not the only one struggling. The challenges can be family related, a medical problem, addiction, mental health and more. They might know intellectually that others have problems too, but to hear that others have serious problems like you can be comforting in a strange way.

I want people to realize that drugs and/or alcohol are not the solution to their problems. It is a chemical substance that will become the food you crave and literally need to prevent severe withdrawal symptoms. The same chemical your body is craving will destroy your organs.

Resilience, courage and faith are three important factors that helped me not just to survive my life, but learn how to live life. It is a process that takes a lot of time and effort.

I learned that it is through adversity that growth occurs. For change to occur (positive and negative) there must be movement and/or action.

My dear mother used to tell me, "If you put the same effort into your school studies as you do into getting alcohol there is no stopping you." As usual she was right.

Instead of continuing to wallow in the self-pity of the past (which cannot be changed), rather than worry and obsess about the future, I suggest that people focus most in the present to change their future. After all, the present time is the only time frame that we have control of. We must be proactive and work to make things different and better.

Have you ever seen that grimy green stuff on pond water while out in the country on a hot sunny day? The algae are there because the water is stagnant. This explains the earlier years of my life. I was stagnant! I sat around, drank, and complained about how terrible my life was while doing nothing to change it.

I had a list in my head and sounded like a broken record when reviewing all of the injustices done to me, all of the unfair things that were happening to me, how I was treated differently than others and was not equipped to do what was needed to change.

Today, when I hear my patients doing this, I validate their frustrations and then ask them what they are doing to change their situation. For those that are honest with themselves and with me, the look on their face is priceless. They give that half grin like a kid caught with their hand in the cookie jar and answer "nothing." They are complaining about their circumstances but are doing nothing to change the situation they are complaining about.

My hopes are that readers can gain insight from my story, particularly recovering from my many diagnoses including alcoholism. What my recovery consists of might be different from yours. What has worked for me may not work for you. But, I encourage everyone to try some of the suggestions because you have nothing to lose and much to gain.

Outcomes are not promised for that reason but my primary goals in sharing my story is to educate, inspire, motivate and instill hope for your future. Rise to the occasion and take the high road as I did. I like the view a lot better and you will too.

The names used in my book have been changed or given initials to protect their identity. I have done so to protect their identity, but many are special to me and you know who you are. A heart felt thank you to my consultant and friend, Rochelle Sufrin, of Sufrin Communications and Strategic Planning. Your encouragement and guidance helped me to write this book, and for giving me the title of the book. The information, dates and many other details are included to the best of my ability and are the way I remember it today.

SECTION I

Problems, Problems, Problems

Living with Epilepsy

Epilepsy is a neurological disorder that results in seizure activity. The definition of seizure as used in the legal term, referred to as a "search and seizure" means, to capture or take possession of. Well, that explains very accurately my experience with epilepsy. Every time I had a Grand Mal seizure, it was violent and captured the freedom of my body, muscles and consciousness and held me prisoner from 1-3 minutes. I had many seizures at a frequent rate, and they were debilitating and traumatic.

Self-esteem and self-image develop at a young age, and mine was poor from the start. The seizures were bad but worse were the social repercussions. They would prove to be far more costly and hurtful because as most already know, kids can be vicious and adults too.

There was also the fear factor. Every seizure was so terrifying that I often wondered if I was possessed by the devil or if something evil was happening to me. I couldn't imagine that something this scary and debilitating could be just a medical problem but more like an exorcism where a demonic force was possessing my body and my mind.

I thought I was living a nightmare and that nightmare was a medical diagnosis of Tuberous Sclerosis Complex. The National Institute of Health describes it as a genetic health condition that consists of many benign tumors throughout the body and in the brain. It can cause major problems with many different organs in the body, learning disabilities, severe depression, behavior problems and severe seizures. I have learned to control my behavior and have been seizure-free for many years but still struggle with the other conditions of Tuberous Sclerosis.

I had, on average, twelve Grand Mal seizures a day and could have as many as thirty to fifty in a day. The medical terminology has changed and today they are known as Tonic Clonic seizures. I had less severe seizures known as Petty and Petit Mal seizures as well. The seizures resulted in countless lacerations and stitches, head injuries and worse.

To give some perspective, please close your eyes. Think about a time when you were either in a deep sleep or were extremely intoxicated or in an unconscious state. Suddenly, your eyes open and you awaken. When you gain your faculties, your eyes are covered, and you can't see a thing. You then realize that you are in excruciating pain. Your forehead and hip are both hurting badly. You try to move but can't. You think, "What the heck is going on? What's happened to me? Something is wrong".

You then realize that your forehead and hip are not on the soft mattress of your bed but on a hard surface. You are on the floor. You tell yourself, "Okay, that explains the pain but why can't I see when my eyes are open, and I am awake?" Now you realize that it is because you are in a dark room and lying face down with your forehead and nose flush against the floor. "Oh man! I must have had a seizure."

You have a terrible headache and are struggling to get off the floor because your hip is injured. You put your hand where it hurts and feel the egg-size lump on your forehead. You limp across the room to turn on the light and look in the mirror. You have to look twice because you don't know what you are looking at because you are still confused from the seizure.

You look a second time and get scared because you look deformed. The swelling is an egg-size lump from your unconscious dead body weight falling, and your head defenselessly and violently hitting the floor. You think you're looking at a cyclops and then realize it is you with a humongous hematoma on your forehead.

Even though you are limping because of the injury to your hip, it seems like nothing after seeing your head. You are concerned that everyone will think the injuries are because you were drunk or lost a fight they'll assume you were in. If I tell them that it was because I had a seizure, they won't believe me and will think I am using my epilepsy as an excuse for being drunk and getting hurt.

Keep in mind that this was only one experience when I have had thousands of seizures over a period of thirty-four years. This doesn't mean that every time I had a seizure I was injured. There were other times when the seizures caused injuries that were significantly worse. Injury or not, when I had a Grand Mal seizure, the fear that preceded unconsciousness was terrifying every time.

The physical trauma was terrible but the social and psychological effects from my seizures were even worse. Unlike physical injury, psychological injury is not visible like the huge egg on my forehead was. There are likely to be many people I have known since I was a child who are not aware that I even had seizures, let alone the repercussions from it.

I was just three years old when I had my first seizure and fell 10-12 feet from the living room window and crashed into the cement driveway. Countless times, I would seize while asleep and fall out of bed as just described. When I awakened, I would be lying between my bed and the wall. Injuries could be a typical egg-size lump on my head or a badly bruised chin and blood in my mouth and on the floor. My brother and I had bunk beds and mine was at the lower level for this reason.

I liked to suck my thumb when I was a kid and countless times, I literally bit my thumb to the bone. Sucking the inside of my cheek was another way I would comfort myself. On several occasions, I had a seizure and bit off the inside of my cheek. When I regained consciousness, my mouth was full of blood and flesh from the inside of my cheek that was making me choke.

I panicked as I choked until my airway was cleared from the blood and flesh that was blocking it. I can remember the tremendous fear as soon as I was alert enough to realize what was happening. I can remember every detail. The thought of it still impacts me today.

My poor mom was taking me to the emergency room at least a half a dozen times every year. She tried her best to prevent me from being injured. From the very beginning, my mother made me promise to follow a strict routine every time I knew that I was about to have a seizure. She presented it as teamwork where each of us had our own responsibilities.

I was very fortunate to have an aura before I seized because some of us with epilepsy do not. The aura was the first stage of my seizures. It was my warning sign that soon I would become terrorized, unconscious, spastic and shake violently. An aura can present differently for different people. My aura felt like I was on an elevator going up very fast and then stopping at a desired floor.

Mom made me promise that when I had the aura, I would yell "Seizure!!!" and then, immediately, get on my bed or the couch and put a pillow in my mouth. If I were out in public, and near dirt or grass, I was to sit or lay down to minimize the risk of injury.

Even when I played it safe and did everything right, there were always consequences. There might be different degrees of severity but almost always there were migraine headaches, exhaustion and soreness throughout my body. But, just as I could count on these intense symptoms, I could count on my sweet and loving mother to be there every time to help me through it.

I remember her having my head in her lap while reassuring me that everything would be okay. She would sing softly to me while running her fingers through my hair that was soaked with sweat. I would slowly cool down and calm down, and mom would stay with me until I fell asleep.

A few times a year, I would just be so tired of being controlled by these seizures that I would just sob. Mom was with me all the way and would rock me back and forth until I calmed down and fell asleep. This was tough on my teammate as well. On several occasions, when I awakened, I would hear mom crying in the other room. I never told her but knew that she was being strong for me whenever she was with me and thoughtfully waiting until I was safe and asleep before she let her feelings out.

My mother was my hero and my protector. I carried so much guilt because I knew that this was consuming her as it was me. This was why I had a lot of fears when I got my first apartment. I would have to live without the protection and security of my mom.

Early on, I had to wear a football helmet because the seizures were so violent. I had become an escape artist by the time I was three or four years old. This was a potentially dangerous combination. My thoughtful and creative mother tied her left leg to my right so she would awaken if I had a seizure or tried to leave the house while she was asleep.

I will preface that it was 1964 when I had my first seizure, and times were different back then. My parents did things that would be considered child abuse these days. The excess fence used to enclose our backyard was placed over the top of my crib and secured with a rope to keep me in the crib for my safety. Who knows what the child abuse charges or the sentence for this act would be today, but this was the best thing they could think of to protect me from serious injury or even death.

The energy expended while having seizures was the equivalent of playing an entire full court basketball game to 10, and I was having twelve of them a day. The seizures were often followed by an hour nap and not because I wanted it but because my mind and body needed it. I had severe migraine headaches too. In my younger years, I would lose my urine and even defecate when I had a seizure. When the seizure ended, I was dazed and confused. Although I knew none of this was my fault, the shame and embarrassment felt, worsened my already poor self-esteem.

You may wonder how I could know all these details if I was unconscious. Well, that's because my mother documented all that she observed and talked to me about it. I was a very curious kid and asked a lot of questions. Mom thought it was important for me to be informed about my illness so that I could educate others if/when needed.

My mother also had a list of questions for the doctor when we went for routine visits to the neurologist and the trips to the emergency room. I watched her as she stood in front of the door (knowingly or not). She must have known because she would not allow my doctor to leave until he had answered and clarified all her questions. It was then and only then that he would be free to go.

Mom made me promise that the first thing I would do is tell the lifeguard that I had seizures when I went to swim so he/she could keep a closer eye on me. I may not have listened to my mom about everything, but this is something I listened to and always took seriously.

Strangely enough seizures were not the worst part of the disorder. To put it bluntly, people can be and quite often are heartless and ignorant. People in general, but particularly children, can be very mean and hurtful. The way I was treated by others helped mold me into the angry and depressed kid that I was becoming. The first time I was called a "seizure boy", I was hurt and cowered. I went home and cried.

I had been called names like "seizure boy" and "pill boy." About the third time I heard one of these names, in plain terms, I beat the hell out of the person who said it. I took it to the next level and made an announcement as I stood over the kid I had just beaten up. I said loudly and angrily that anyone who made fun of me for having seizures or taking medication would pay the same price or worse. I wanted everyone to have a fair warning and know that they would regret teasing and bullying me.

It wasn't very common to see a first grader standing at the water fountain taking pills, but by six years old, I knew all about my seizures, what medications I was taking, how many of them to take and what time I was to take them. Rather than being commended for being a responsible child, I was made fun of. Whether these names were intended to hurt or not, they certainly did. These kids didn't know, but they were creating a mean and angry boy.

Word got around quickly that I was a "nut" and that no one should "mess with me" as we used to say. My reaction to being bullied proved a blessing and a curse. On the one hand, it was a blessing because it worked, and I was seldom made fun of after that. On the other hand, it was a curse because I learned early that being angry, violent and intimidating worked. This gave me a false sense of control because I was slowly but surely losing control.

When there wasn't the name calling, there was the not so subtle whispering and being looked at like I had the plague. I remember getting along with kids and maybe even being liked by them, but once they saw me fall to the ground, stiffen and shake uncontrollably while my face was contorted and saliva drooled from my mouth, things often would change. I could understand how scary it was for them.

Their often cold and alienating response had me thinking, "Then just imagine what it's like for me". Many people have treated me very differently after seeing me have a seizure. They were not comfortable being around me. In response, I would snap at them and call them out because they were being phony. I would tell them that if they ever talked to me again or acted like they were my friend, I would knock them out. I felt better because they would stay away from me for fear of being beat up. For a while thereafter, I would give them a dirty look and scare the hell out of them. Doing this made me feel better because it was making them uncomfortable.

Then there were those who responded with the other extreme. They would treat me like I was hopeless and incapable. By then, I had been living with this disability for several years. I knew they meant well and I appreciated their sympathy and willingness to support me, but that wasn't what I wanted either. The fact was, no one really understood me or could comfort me.

I was a very good athlete and played basketball all the time when I was younger. I can remember being on the court and feeling a seizure about to occur. The aura (warning that a seizure is coming) would occur, and I would tell a teammate that a seizure was coming on, and I would go sit against the fence.

When I regained my faculties, I would look up and several people would be standing almost on top of me asking if the paramedics should be called. I thought, it's a good thing that I don't need the paramedics because everyone is just standing there. However, there were other times when someone did call for help, which was the right thing to do as a precaution. But that wasn't what I wanted or needed, either. I didn't need it unless I was injured, so I would decline going to the hospital.

I knew the person meant well, and I knew I was being unreasonable thinking that they would know what to do. To be fair, I neither expected nor wanted anyone to begin running their fingers through my sweaty hair like mom did because they were not my mom. Only she responded perfectly and gave me just what I needed when I needed it. I can't explain how or why, but she always did. I think the seizures were "our thing." It was the one thing that we worked at together for as far back as I can remember.

My own father didn't know exactly what to do, although I know he did his best. I remember hanging out with dad one day. I woke up in the Intensive Care Unit at a local hospital. I found out later, that I had a seizure, and my dad said that he thought it had stopped, and then it went on to become one seizure after another. This is called Status Epilepticus.

I was told I had one seizure after another, and they did not stop for about thirty minutes. My late neurologist had told me that Status Epilepticus can be life threatening and that I was lucky to be alive, based on what my father had witnessed.

My mother was so angry at my father because he stayed with me and didn't call for help. He explained that he stayed to protect me from injury because he was expecting the seizures to stop. My mother was angry at him because not calling for help earlier put my life at risk. I defended my dad and explained that he did what he thought was right and how much I appreciated him protecting me. He didn't know what was going on like she does. He felt bad and said that he would have called for help earlier if he had known better.

The painful thing that I learned early on is that having epilepsy would make it difficult, if not impossible, for me to fit in. Because the seizures were so severe, I was in and out of the hospital all the time. Even when the seizures would become somewhat controlled, I still had to go and have Magnetic Resonance Imaging (MRIs), Electroencephalograms (EEGs), Computed Tomography (CT) scans and Positron Emission Tomography (PET) scans.

This always reminded me of how different I was because I didn't know any other kids in my school who would be there one minute and gone the next. They were present throughout the entire school year. Even kids who got sick returned in good health. I always had something going on and something always seemed wrong, just because of the ongoing testing.

The other thing was that I already had ADHD which is a developmental disability that includes cognitive deficits which caused barriers to doing well in school. I already had to attend special education classes but could never really catch on or catch up because I did not attend school consistently. When it wasn't the testing, it was inpatient hospitalizations from serious injuries incurred from seizures. I was often suspended for behavior problems and acting out because I was always so angry and frustrated.

I hated the EEGs most because the test consisted of around thirty wires that were placed in specific areas on my head. The purpose was to observe brain waves and brain activity. What I hated was the glue-like substance that was used to make sure that the wires stuck to the scalp. It didn't seem to matter how many times I shampooed my hair, days later, I would go to school and classmates would ask what was in my hair.

Do I tell them that it's from an EEG because I have seizures or do I let them assume that I was a dirty kid who never washed his hair? It was another reason for kids to talk behind my back. I know some felt bad for me, and others thought I was a strange kid who had poor hygiene. I knew a lot of this could be my own insecurities but that's what I was thinking and feeling. Even at a young age, I could read people reasonably well. I frequently wondered why I had to be different, and it was depressing and frustrating.

There are many other examples of abuse I could give, and one that comes to mind is an encounter I had with the police. It was a typical day. This means that I had spent my day drinking and was severely intoxicated. I talked with a slur, and I was staggering down the street.

A police officer pulled over and stopped. As he got out of the car and approached me, I fell to the ground and began flopping all over the place. Having a seizure while sloshed was very uncommon. In my heavy drinking days, the seizures most often came when I was in withdrawal from alcohol. But, I was having a full-blown seizure and friends who witnessed this, later told me that the officer assumed I was being uncooperative by not following his commands.

A friend later explained that the officer yelled at me emphatically and dragged me toward his car. He said it was obvious to him that I was having a seizure and couldn't understand how the police officer didn't realize that. He also explained that the brush burns to my face were because I was lying face down while seizing, and the officer lifted my feet and dragged my face along the street.

I am not asking anyone to condone my behavior in these situations, I just hope that people understand what abuse does to people and the monster I was because of it. I think about this incident and many others where I exercised poor judgment and self-destructive behaviors. I used people hurting me, my disabilities, and alcoholism as an excuse but as you can see, I was held accountable for sure.

These encounters and past mistakes have created "counseling" or "teaching" moments for clients I have worked with over the years. I call it "distinguishing the two Es". I try to help them see that the problems (addiction, victim of abuse) might help to *explain* the behaviors exhibited but it does not *excuse* them. The bottom line is that life is about decisions and choices that we make, and there are consequences for all of them. The fact is, most of the time, I reacted in ways that made things worse for me.

With that said, I stopped drinking when I was 36 years of age. I have learned how to cope and manage stress much better over the years. Most importantly, I have learned to minimize it and sometimes prevent it from occurring in the first place. For example, I have cut certain people out of my life because they are disrespectful, demeaning or just plain negative. My father used to tell me that you must treat certain people like you would treat cancer and cut them out of your life.

Life is too short, and in hindsight, I wasted many years being sad and angry because of my problems and the way I was treated because of them. Today, I surround myself with people who genuinely care about me and enhance my life. I have been seizure-free for a long time but still choose to take medication/s to prevent the seizures from returning.

I have stayed connected and spent a lot of time over the years with the Epilepsy Foundation. I have been a support on their web page for those that still struggle with seizures and the abundance of other problems that come with it. I volunteered to answer questions sent by people struggling with epilepsy because I have experienced and worked through many of the same issues.

I have attended events to stay involved and have been a keynote and motivational speaker and shared my experiences as an epileptic. I also presented information regarding the correlation between neurological illnesses like: Cerebral Palsy (CP), Epilepsy, Intermittent Explosive Disorder (IED), poor impulse control, addiction and depression.

Please be thoughtful about what you say and do to others. You can influence people's lives, whether it be positive or negative. You can bring a smile to their face and a light into their dark world without even knowing it. When you are being mean and unthoughtful, you could be making that dark world even darker, and you might be creating a monster.

Living with Attention Deficit Hyperactivity Disorder

As a child, I was diagnosed with Attention Deficit Disorder (ADD) as it was called then. Later, they added hyperactivity to the diagnosis. You can be diagnosed with or without hyperactivity. Adding the hyperactivity was certainly accurate and justifiable with me. Although most children have a lot of energy, I had an inordinate amount. Apparently, to an abnormal degree, and could not sit still for any length of time.

Attention Deficit Hyperactivity Disorder (ADHD) consists of a variety of symptoms or factors that include behaviors and cognitive deficits. We have difficulty getting focused and staying focused for extended periods. We have difficulty processing information and often, do poorly in school without tutoring and guidance to stay on task.

When we ask a question, a teacher, parent or friend better answer it quickly or we will be challenging for those who deal with us on a regular basis. To reiterate, I know that many children behave like this but when you have ADHD you do these things to extremes, and they impact your ability to function significantly.

Impulse control and violence can be part of the ADHD behaviors as well. We are tightly wound and often frustrated by all the confusion going on in our heads. It's not uncommon for us to take our frustrations out on others. When you add being made fun of by peers or being demeaned by family members, the results can be violent behavior due to anger, frustration and poor impulse control.

I have always had trouble completing one thing before moving on to another. Before I complete one project, I have begun two more. The next thing I know, I have three projects that are incomplete. In order to complete any of these, let alone all of them, someone must point this out to me. Sometimes, I must remove myself from the task at hand and then return later to finish what I started.

In my elementary school years, classmates seemed to be far more intelligent than I. They didn't seem to be struggling like I was. Unlike me, they could sit still in the classroom and focus on the reading assignment. Like me, however, they had the energy to play when it came time for recess. They could do both, I could not.

If I sat still, I could not stay focused because my thoughts were racing. Extra efforts were made to concentrate without success. Then came frustration and a sense of hopelessness. When the teachers asked what we just read, my classmates could describe in detail what they had just read while I sat there confused and wondering how they came up with those details when I didn't have a clue after reading the same thing.

Other times, I would look up to see that I was only half done while other students were having side conversations while waiting for me to get done.

With ADHD the one thing you learn early on is that children are cruel. I might have been a slow learner with reading, but I learned quickly how mean kids can be. There's a lack of awareness of the damage they are doing to their peer/s by bullying them and making fun of them.

For kids born with the natural ability to process information and remain attentive, they cannot understand how someone can struggle with things that come so easily to them. They often take these gifts for granted. Young people begin positioning themselves regarding who is part of the popular crowd; who is the best looking, the smartest, the best athlete and so on . . .?

By second grade, I was placed in special education classes and assigned to Room #14 with the other children who had learning disabilities. The other students often referred to us as "The Room #14 idiots." How's that for self-esteem and encouragement? I already had a lot going on with my own internal battles about being "slow". Words like retarded, depressed and oppressed, slow, down and low were used to refer to us. When it came to kids establishing and positioning themselves as I mentioned earlier, I was near the bottom of the totem pole for academic reasons, but also because I was a hot head and had seizures. I was popular though with the cut-ups and ball players.

I hated homework when I was in elementary school and high school. I did enough to get through and to pass from grade to grade. The ADHD prevented my head from being into my studies. So, my heart could not be in it. I knew that I couldn't learn at the same pace as those in regular classes, but also knew I had more potential than some who were in special education with me. Some of us, in Room #14, were also in mainstream classes.

Quite honestly, I never felt that I belonged in either of them. To many students in the mainstream classes, I was a Room #14 idiot. The reason this expression hurt so much is I believed it to some degree. This, coupled with my epilepsy, for which I was also made fun of, evoked a lot of anger. The anger was both internal and external. From early on, there was a lot of self-loathing and acting out.

If I was going to be seen or treated as an outcast, then so be it. That was my attitude. I turned to violence at an early age. When someone referred to me as a "Room #14 idiot" or "seizure boy" or "pill boy", I retaliated by beating the hell out of them. I kind of enjoyed it because I believed that someone had to be evil to say unkind things to people with disabilities. That bully deserved to be beaten up as far as I was concerned.

I found out that beating people up eventually worked because they stopped making fun of me. This told me at an early age, that violence works and is the answer to this problem. But, with that comes a lot of consequences.

The inability to control my temper resulted in lost friendships, (later going to jail), a bad reputation and feeling even worse about myself because I knew I was out-of-control. I also have a conscience, and every time I assaulted someone, I felt bad. Like drugs and alcohol, assaulting the bully felt good at that moment, but shortly thereafter, I felt bad because I had hurt another human being.

While in my early twenties, I enrolled at a small school for the disabled. During lunch break, an ignorant peer said something offensive, and I confronted him about it. The argument escalated, and he raised his fist to punch me. I came at him full force, with my forehead, and head-butted him, and literally, smashed his nose. When my forehead made contact, blood squirted everywhere. He was dazed and screaming in pain when I grabbed him and took him to the ground. I punched him a few more times, and then held him to the ground. The fight was over quickly, and so was my college experience at that school.

The school policy was that any students involved in physical violence would be expelled from the school. This was not determined by who was right or wrong. Whoever was involved, (right or wrong), was immediately expelled. Whether I thought that was right or wrong didn't matter because both of us were packing up and going back home. This was an opportunity to get a college education and start a new life, but I was not ready and did not have control of myself or my anger enough to complete that schooling.

There were a few key reasons why I didn't care about getting kicked out. First, I thought that he had started the fight and got what he deserved. Second, even if I didn't have problems with anger, I was brought up to defend myself. If someone started a fight with me, I would try to be the finisher. Lastly, I still wanted to drink more than I wanted to study and be away from my dysfunctional family and friends, and that is probably why I didn't care about the consequences.

I was still drinking heavily at the time, so there was little chance of me getting control even if I wanted to. A lot of these problems and behaviors stemmed from my home life, ADHD, alcohol abuse and epilepsy. They are all contributing factors to my anger management and impulse control problems. This might explain the behavior but is no excuse for losing control and beating people up, whether I believe they deserve it or not. It is my responsibility to do what it takes to get control, whether it be therapy, medication or any other alternatives.

In my earlier years, my father often became frustrated with me because he had to tell me things repeatedly. I also was a curious kid and asked a lot of questions. Whether it was my curiosity, asking because I forgot, didn't understand or was just confused, having to explain or repeat himself was very frustrating for him. Though I understood his frustration, he did not seem to understand mine.

Over the years, dad asked me more than once, "Are you playing dumb just so I don't ask you to help me anymore?" I couldn't understand why he would ask this because I wanted nothing more than to please my dad. My father was born in 1926 and served in WWII. This was not the generation to ask "Why?", whether it's because you are curious or because you are confused due to having ADHD. The answer is still "Because I said so that's why."

To date, even as a professional clinician, I struggle with some of the daily responsibilities that require being organized, having concentration and remembering things I have been told. I sometimes see the frustration in colleagues when I ask about something that has been answered or explained several times.

I'm thinking, "Yeah, tell me about it. I must live with it every day". What I have also seen over the years is that I can live with ADHD and still be very good at my job. I can excel and be appreciated for the skills and strengths I contribute.

When I first met my wife, I found that she had earned a Master's degree in Library Science and did so with a learning disability. At the young age of five, her kindergarten teacher said that she was mentally retarded. Both of her parents knew this was not so and had her evaluated by a school psychologist who determined that she was dyslexic.

She, too, struggled early in school, but unlike me, in later grades, she was in gifted and advanced classes in several subjects. Unlike me, who barely passed my GED, she excelled despite her learning disability.

We have had entirely different journeys, but ended up at the same level of education, from the same university and now are living in the same home for the rest of our lives. This was very refreshing to me because I never thought that I could achieve even a fraction of what I have. I attended public schools at various times. Seven of my 11 ½ years of school were while living in juvenile institutions. At seventeen years of age, I graduated while living in a juvenile institution. I barely passed the GED test but was finally done with school or so I thought.

To this day, there are things that other people were exposed to in school that I was not, and that I am still ignorant about. I have also found that though I am lacking in many areas, living through those experiences have made me stronger in ways that good students and those without disabilities will never know about.

When talking about my ADHD, I can't help but think about the expressions, "God has a sense of humor" and "God works in mysterious ways". The humor is that I hated reading when I was a kid because I wasn't good at it, and it created too much frustration for me. So, what happened?

Years later, I chose social work as my major at the University of Pittsburgh. The major I chose would require reading between 300-500 or more pages every week for study. I came to love it and became pretty good at reading, taking notes and writing according to my professors. I may not have believed them, but I got very good grades in college.

Despite all my academic struggles, after seven years of college, I earned an Associate Degree in Criminal Justice at the Community College of Allegheny County and a Bachelor's and Master's Degree in Social Work at the University of Pittsburgh. It is one of the top ranked Schools of Social Work in the country. That is pretty darn good for a Room #14 idiot as *they* used to call me. I went from "a Room #14 idiot" to a Master of Social Work, a counselor, a psychotherapist, a teacher, a trainer, a motivational speaker and now, a published author. Not too shabby.

My many diagnoses and disabilities have given me insight and life experiences that enable me to be more compassionate and understanding as a psychotherapist. I am less judgmental of others. I know that what others might see as a flaw or a deficit can become a strength and a blessing in disguise. As a counselor, knowing these things leaves room for a glimmer of hope when my clients see no hope.

To anyone with a learning disability, I say, "Please don't give up". There is far more support, expertise and resources for those with ADHD than there were many years ago. If you need a tutor, get one! If you need help, ask for it! Many schools have accommodations for students these days and try to help you to succeed. However, there are still the bullies out there who have a need to make you feel worse so that they can feel better.

Keep your head up and understand that you are not dumb, stupid or an idiot! You are a person with potential who has some barriers that you must fight through to achieve what comes far easier to others. Classmates and others can give you such labels, but you don't have to wear that label or identify with that label.

I am proud to say that my wife and I are examples of people with learning disabilities (ADHD and Dyslexia) who have achieved success despite the barriers, the labels and discouragement felt at times. We have earned Master's Degrees in Social Work and Library of Science from the University of Pittsburgh because we chose to do what was necessary to achieve our goals. We must work harder to achieve the same success.

However, working through feelings of hopelessness, frustration and even thoughts of giving up are what made it that much sweeter when I finally accomplished my goals. The same goals that I thought could only happen in a dream. This is what makes achieving the goal more special and meaningful.

I remember literally, crying myself to sleep on more than one occasion, thinking that there was no way I would be able to graduate from community college, and I had similar moments while studying for my Bachelor's and Master's degrees. Yes, a grown man in his thirties was crying himself to sleep due to discouragement and doubt about being able to complete college successfully.

It took classmates a fraction of the time to complete the same project as I. But the bottom line was, on graduation day, we were all walking across the same stage and receiving the same degree. That would not have happened had I given in to my doubts, given up and not worked extra hard.

Please remember to keep your head up, and don't be ashamed of your disability. Instead, allow it to motivate you to work harder and longer to achieve the same result. If you continued to battle through all the challenges and barriers that come with having ADHD and other learning disabilities, you are destined to be successful.

Living with Clinical Depression

I am a Social Worker today and work as a counselor. For that, I am happy and eternally grateful. However, my first 36 years were like living a nightmare because it was so full of chaos, violence and clinical depression. The last 21 years have become easier every year, but I still must meet with my trauma therapist to address the Post Traumatic Stress Disorder (PTSD) and Major Depressive Disorder (MDD) so that I can function and keep my job.

The symptoms of clinical depression consist of: depressed mood, suicidal and/or homicidal ideations, feelings of hopelessness and helplessness, anhedonia (lack of interest), poor libido, extreme changes in sleep, (one extreme or the other) poor sleep or too much sleep, extremes with weight loss and gain and/or increased or decreased appetite, somatic complaints and cognitive deficits with concentration, comprehension and memory.

Clinical depression is common with those like me, people with **neurological** problems like epilepsy. My depression was the result of, and/or correlated with, the seizures and cognitive deficits that come with epilepsy and ADHD diagnoses. As explained earlier, depression is also common among those with Tuberous Sclerosis Complex. Being alienated and picked on by peers contributed to poor self-esteem and severe depression that I have lived with since my very early years in life.

I remember being sad a lot when I was just five or six years old because my parents got divorced when I was three. My oldest brother moved down to Kentucky and lived with our grandparents for about three years while my middle brother and I lived in the projects with our mother.

I frequently thought and felt like I was helpless with my seizures and that made me very sad. I sometimes was afraid to go to sleep for fear of having a seizure and waking up on the floor after falling out of bed. I felt sorry for myself a lot. All these things made me feel like I was less than everyone else. It made me feel worthless and served only to intensify my sadness.

The longer these things went on with little to no improvement, the more helpless and depressed I felt. Being poor and living in an oppressed environment, like the Rankin Projects' Hawkins Village, was not a situation or a lifestyle that would improve my mood either. Even after getting out of the projects and moving to a much better neighborhood, I remained very sad but for many new reasons.

During the time we lived in the projects, my father picked us up for the weekend and returned us to my mom for school during the week. I missed him so much. He was my hero. During that period, I could only see him for a limited amount of time and then we had to return to

Building C, of the Rankin, Pennsylvania Projects, known as Hawkins Village.

We wanted to get out of the projects and live with my father because my mother could not afford better housing at the time. She was a stay-at-home mom before my parents divorced. My mother was extremely wise and intelligent but only had a high school diploma at that time. This meant that her employment opportunities were limited. I felt so guilty because I didn't want to leave her, but they had decided it was time to be with dad.

Dad was better off financially but could not provide the bond or meet my internal needs the way my mom could. I was also frightened because mom was my protector. She knew how to handle anything and everything. Quite frankly, I was very excited at the thought of a new home to live in and having my eldest sibling return from Kentucky after being away for several years. I was also frightened because I knew I wouldn't see my mother very often.

I was no longer with mom and that was depressing. Mom was the only one that knew how to comfort me and handle situations with my seizures. I knew other family members loved me, but no one could show it and make me feel loved like my mother. She was part of my soul and was the only one in the world that knew what I needed and when I needed it.

After all, I had been with her the first six years of my life, and we had already been through a lot together with the seizures, tough times and one transition after the next, including this one. It was not easy for any of us but that was how it was. My dad was giving up his freedoms and taking on three kids that he never really had to take care of before. That was my mom's "job" when they were married and after their divorce. Dad was primarily the breadwinner.

He would now be taking on three kids who were six, seven and eleven years old while working full-time. This was a big change for him. He asked his mother for help and my grandmother moved in. She would take on the housework, cooking and a lot of the yelling, hugging and kissing. There was a lot of all of that.

We got out of the projects when my father bought a house. It was a very nice neighborhood and my eldest brother came back from

Kentucky. All three of us were back together. My grandmother moved in with us so that she could take care of us and the housework, while my father worked as a police officer for the City of Pittsburgh.

For a very brief period, we were in a happy and celebratory mode but that didn't last because early on, the arguing and fighting began. It appears we were all trying to compete for my father's love. My father did not have the patience that my mother did, and he did not communicate with me as my mother did. For example, if I asked mom a question she would sit down and explain it to me. She was happy that I was curious about things and wanted to know about them. My father, on the other hand, was from the "old school" and did not like being asked questions all the time.

He was born in 1926 and was from what many consider the Greatest Generation that ever lived. However, with that Greatest Generation came a lot of flaws and insensitivities. I believe that we have become a far too sensitive society today. Dad was the other extreme. He seemed to feel burdened when I asked a question, and this made me feel like a burden. He was one of those guys that when we asked why, his expression was, "Because I said so. That's why". There was the all too popular, "Children should be seen and not heard". This was in great contrast to the open communication that was welcomed by mom. This told me that she valued me, and what I had to say.

My dad didn't understand that at the young age of six, my self-image was that of a dumb epileptic whom no one loved or cared about, except my mother. I'm not sure if he was incapable of communicating with a child for some reason. This is in stunning contrast to the way my mom and I talked. But even with her, I was generally unhappy because of our situation. If it wasn't for our special relationship, the many different factors mentioned would have been even more depressing.

Keep in mind that a white family living in the projects in the 1960s made us the minority. Even today, when I mention that some of my history was spent living in the Rankin Projects,' Hawkins Village, I get a look of surprise and disbelief. During that era, being divorced was considered shameful like collecting green stamps. They were then what food stamps are today. I was too young to contemplate suicide but remember being unhappy and feeling like an outcast in yet another way.

Now I was with my dad and living in a much nicer area and had far more but was just as depressed for different reasons. The aloof and cold responses were just the beginning. My depression increased but was not as recognizable because it was masked with anger. I began to lash back, and dad wasn't going to have any part of that. It got to the point that when he was mean and yelled at me, I yelled back. When he hit me, I hit him back and then it got even worse, but I didn't care.

The older I got, the more depressed I became. My anger and resentment grew more and more every day. Before I knew it, I was spending a lot of time in hospitals for attempting suicide, injuries from seizures and from fighting when I was drunk. I hated life more and more every day, and my parents did not know what to do.

When I look back now, I had so much practice at being sad and feeling sorry for myself that I became a pro at it and did it without trying. I learned to see life through the eyes of a victim. I had many reasons for this. I was a victim of abuse, bullying and much more but didn't learn until years later, that until I empowered myself and changed my life, I would remain a hopeless and helpless victim who was sad and angry more often than not. Today, I look at the few pictures I have from my childhood and most, if not all of them, show a sad kid. I see a very sad boy with an injured soul.

I remember like it was yesterday when I had finally had enough. I had been depressed for several years by the time I was nine years old. I had been wishing I was dead for many days in a row. All I could think about was that I wanted it all to be over. I thought that the only way to achieve that was to kill myself. I had thought about it before, but this time was different. Instead of thinking about it occasionally, I couldn't get it off my mind. I wanted to end it all.

My one experience with attempting suicide with a gun occurred when I was just nine years old. Dad owned several guns, and I knew that he kept one of them in the drawer of the end table next to his bed. Grandma was at the store. Both of my brothers were out doing whatever, and dad was at work. If I was going to do anything, this was the time. I walked into his room and opened the drawer, and there it was. I picked it up and looked at it. I lifted it toward my head but couldn't do it. When I realized this, my sadness turned to anger. I screamed at the top of my lungs, wiped the tears from my face, threw the gun back into the drawer and went back to my miserable life.

In my younger years, I would take 20 or 30 pills when attempting suicide. As I got older, I began taking more and more and washing them down with alcohol. The closest to dying was a time when I had taken a new prescription and guzzled a liter of vodka. I was taking six 100 mg Dilantin capsules a day normally, so I had one hundred and eighty of them.

I decided I was done with all the physical and verbal battles. I was tired of battling with life itself. As I had told myself many times before, I was putting an end to this hell once and for all. I walked over to my dresser where my new full prescription bottle was. I thought to myself, "I'm sorry mom but life will be better off for you without me anyway. Dad hates me and I hate him, so there will be no loss there".

I twisted the top off the big bottle, tilted my head back and poured about sixty pills into my mouth. I freely poured the vodka into my mouth and could feel the big lump of pills sliding down my throat. It felt like I was going to choke, so I hurried and guzzled more and more vodka until my air-pipe and chest were cleared. I poured a bunch more pills into my mouth followed by more big gulps of vodka.

I was becoming more and more disoriented. I knew that I had to go lie down on the bed or I could fall and hurt myself. Yes, one can think weird thoughts when consuming 18,000 milligrams of Dilantin and 1 liter of vodka in about an hour. Here I was trying to kill myself but was concerned that I might hurt myself by falling.

I was looking for any kind of relief I could find and was desperate to get it. I began experimenting with alcohol and marijuana to escape when I was just twelve years old. I was dependent on alcohol to get me from one day to the next by the time I was fifteen years old.

My life was depressing, but what I wasn't told was that alcohol is a depressant as well. Consuming excessive amounts of alcohol would create more problems and more depression. To escape it, I would want more alcohol only to become more depressed. Drinking seemed like fun early on, but I was in the process of self-destructing.

I hated myself and dreaded getting up in the morning. I often had trouble with simple tasks like getting out of bed because I was so depressed and emotionally drained. Once I did get up, I couldn't relax and was always moving around. My mind would race due to the ADHD only to cause more confusion and more difficulty concentrating, comprehending and remembering things. All this confusion, of course, would make me frustrated, angry and ultimately, even more depressed.

I remember one day drinking a pint of Southern Comfort on my way to ninth grade homeroom class. I hated reading class in school because I couldn't concentrate. I would read a page or two and have little to no idea about what I had just read. Consuming a pint of liquor was not a recipe for success in school, of course, but I don't think it made it any worse at that time either. I would have to read things again and again and would get frustrated because my efforts seemed to be useless. I was very impatient and was convinced that things would never improve.

I look at some of my childhood pictures and can't find a smile in any of them. I heard, many years later, that depression is anger turned inward and anger is depression turned outward. There is also the thought that when there is anger, most often there is an underlying feeling. That underlying feeling for me was most often depression.

The verbal abuse was as harmful as the physical abuse. With no exaggeration, I must have been told that, "You're a piece of shit. You're never going to amount to anything. You're a lazy, useless bastard" hundreds, if not thousands of times. These comments only solidified what I was already thinking about myself.

My self-esteem and self-image had been destroyed at a very young age. The more I heard the demeaning comments the more I believed them. I look back now, and it's all so clear how and why I have had clinical depression almost all my life. One of the most common symptoms of depression is irritability.

Tuberous sclerosis already includes many clinical and behavioral symptoms and problems that can be exacerbated by physical, verbal and emotional abuse. This explains why I became a very angry person at a young age. Like so many other things, the anger became progressively worse. This is likely the reason I became a social worker, and why I am drawn to working with patients with co-occurring disorders. Those with co-occurring disorders have many complex issues.

I remember wanting more than anything to get out of bed and just couldn't. I would have loved more than anything to be active and productive. Though sports were my love and my only real positive outlet, there were times when I couldn't even get up to play ball. I remember getting so mad when family members or others would accuse me of trying to "milk the government" because I wanted so bad to have a life that was more than being depressed, drinking, playing sports and collecting a check that I hadn't earned.

At my father's and many other parents' defense, they are ignorant about mental health and/or have never experienced clinical depression. For example, extremes of insomnia or hypersomnia as well feeling fatigued, somatic complaints like aches and pains that are sometimes unexplainable are all relatively common occurrences of clinical depression.

I have grown to believe that someone who can accuse us of being lazy and tell us, "Get your lazy ass out of bed and quit just laying around and doing nothing with your life" can be a frustrated person who loves us. What they are really saying is that they are concerned because you are not living a more productive life. They just have a not so articulate way of putting it.

Before I grew to see it that way, my life involved a lot of arguing, yelling, screaming and fighting with family members and many others who saw me in that light. When it became too much, I tried to escape physically by running away, getting drunk or high or attempting suicide. There was always some kind of battle inside and outside, and we all had enough of it. I was declared "incorrigible" and placed in juvenile institutions for seven years of my life.

For 20 years, I would awaken angry, for the simple reason that I woke up. My first two thoughts were, "Aw f***, I must live another day". My second thought was, "Where am I going to get the booze and weed so I can do that?" I was literally trying to drink my depression away, and more times than not, I was trying to literally drink myself to death. I was drinking myself into oblivion almost every night by consuming a slew of alcohol (which is a depressant) to cope with depression. I wanted to die because I felt stuck and like nothing would ever change.

I thought the world was against me and sometimes couldn't believe there was a God. How could God possibly allow these things to happen to me? I still have depressive episodes, flashbacks and nightmares about being stomped into the ground and having guns put in my face.

My diagnosis of Tuberous Sclerosis Complex cannot be understated because with it came so many other problems. The worst was the epilepsy. Because of the epilepsy, I had many injuries and spent a lot of time in the hospital. The hospital is a very depressing place, particularly for a young kid who wants to be out playing with his friends.

I was in every hospital in the City of Pittsburgh at various times for various reasons. One of the many things that Pittsburgh is known for is the abundance of hospitals and medical care. I was hospitalized at: St. Margaret's, St. Francis, Presbyterian, Forbes Regional, Allegheny General, Mercy, Divine Providence, Montefiore, Shadyside and WPIC (Western Psychiatric Institute and Clinic) for medical and as you can see, mental health problems as well. The only place in my city, I had never been hospitalized was Magee *Women's* Hospital. Times have changed though as they now treat men, and I have been there too.

Many of the psychological problems I had also stemmed from my medical diagnosis because as the NIH had described, it is not uncommon for those with Tuberous Sclerosis Complex to have behavior problems, ADHD and clinical depression. All of these affected my social life.

In addition to being hospitalized, I spent many years in juvenile institutions and even Woodville, which was a state hospital known for the "mentally insane." I tried to keep the mental hospital stays a secret from friends in the neighborhood. Difficult to do when you just up and leave for a month or two with no warning and then suddenly show back up. Everyone already knew I was unstable.

Anger is an issue that is common with people who have neurological problems like epilepsy and cerebral palsy. I had presented a PowerPoint presentation about this at the Epilepsy Foundation of Western Pennsylvania. Staff members who had worked there said that that could be a common occurrence for some of their clients. The fact is many of us with neurological problems like epilepsy and cerebral palsy have impulse control problems. Another factor that had a negative impact on depression and anger was my alcoholism. Alcoholism is known to negatively impact decision making and self-control just as those with major depressive disorder.

This all explains why people with one or two of these problems are at risk of harming themselves or someone else. However, I had not one, not two, but several things that were impacting impulse control and my ability to make good decisions. Worse yet, I got to a point where I didn't even care about the consequences. I didn't think that life could get worse anyhow, so negative consequences carried almost no weight. Life becomes reckless without a deterrent.

There is a term, "suicide by cop." That means that the person will make a gesture like he/she is reaching for a gun when confronted by the police with the hope that the police officer will shoot and kill them. I never actually did this, but I lived a high-risk lifestyle, hoping that I would die in the process.

There was an incident that I remember. It was about 1 AM or 2 AM and I was drunk as usual. I was walking across the street and a car came closer to me than I would have liked, so I kicked the car and put a dent in it. I called the driver some names that mom and dad wouldn't teach their kids. Well, by the time he screeched his tires and got out of the car, he was about 30-40 feet away from me. He responded with a similar choice of words and was not pleased with the dent I had just put in his car with my size 12D shoe.

I suddenly noticed that he had a gun in his hand. He lifted it from his side, pointed it at me and threatened to shoot me. My immediate reaction was fear and anxiety. A split second later, those feelings and emotions turned to anger and disgust. It was as if I reminded myself very quickly that I didn't give a damn and that I wanted to die anyhow because I hated life. So why would I care if he shot and killed me?

I slowly walked toward him. As I did, I told him that he better decide soon because if he didn't shoot me soon enough, I would kill him with my bare hands. The closer I got to him, the angrier I became. I was 10-15 feet from him when he said, "You are fucking crazy!" He threw his gun on to the seat of his car, jumped in and sped off. I yelled and screamed at him as he drove away. It took me a while to cool down.

I was left there alone at a ridiculous hour, and no one was out. With no one to yell at or fight with, I walked home lonely and depressed as usual.

The next day when I woke up and remembered what had happened, I agreed that I was fucking crazy. I also realized that I was still alive and still had to live another day of unhappiness and self-destruction until my eventual demise.

For years, I responded to my depression with poor decisions that only made bad things worse. I learned to use my anger and fears to motivate myself to change my situation or circumstances if that was even possible. I resolved to use the Serenity Prayer that states, "God, *grant me the serenity to accept the things I cannot change,* the courage to change the things I can, and the wisdom to know the difference."

When I reflect on my past, I consistently complained and felt sorry for myself. This only depressed me more. I see the same behaviors with my patients on a regular basis. When I catch myself falling into the complaining or "poor me" mode, the first thing I ask myself is, "Is this something I can change?" If it is, then I figure out a way to do that. If it is something that is out of my control, the best thing to do is accept it.

For example, if I think that I deserve a raise. Instead of complaining that I am not getting the money that I "deserve" for the work I do, the only chance in getting a raise is to request one. Remember, that once I request the raise, the decision is out of my hands. Ask for a raise and if you don't get it, you must accept it and move on.

When you are doing things the right way, in the long run things will work out even if not quite the way you wanted it or planned it. After requesting a raise more than once and being denied, I continued to do my job. I may not have been entirely pleased, but I accepted it and moved on. A couple of years later, I had serious medical problems when I broke seven ribs in ten places.

This was compounded by acquiring sepsis and pneumonia a day or two later. These life-threatening illnesses kept me out of work for two months. The X-Rays, CT scans and MRIs done helped find a tumor on my kidney that I chose to have removed. I had to wait two months until I rebounded from the broken ribs, pneumonia and sepsis, so the tumor and a portion of my kidney could be removed.

I came back to work for two months and then returned to the hospital to have the tumor and a piece of my kidney removed as a precaution. I returned to work after almost another two months. Days after my return I received my paycheck. Ironically, my first paycheck received upon return included a raise in pay.

To summarize, I work hard, ask for a raise and my request is declined. A year or two later, I miss four months in a six month period of work and get a raise days after my return. I try to remember these kinds of things today when I get depressed, angry or discouraged.

If the negative attitude continues, it's likely to create additional problems. Without acceptance, you will stay stuck in the negativity. This will have an impact on your mood, your quality of work, productivity and relationships with co-workers and your employer.

The longer I obsessed about things that made me angry or depressed, the angrier and more depressed I became. This can still happen if I don't catch myself early on and shift my thinking to being grateful for the wonderful life I have today that I never thought possible. My wonderful wife, my job, our home and countless other things can be forgotten.

I think about the many people that lost their homes and their jobs because a company was downsizing. Many have lost their homes to forest fires that have burned everything they own to the ground. There are the floods from hurricanes and much more. Today, they would be grateful to have what many do. By shifting my thoughts to being humble and grateful, my feelings shift from anger or depression to acceptance. It is then that I am ready to move forward.

I encourage everyone with a mental illness to be resilient and use your negative feelings and energy to motivate yourself to improve your situation rather than hinder it. Mental illness is a diagnosis, it's not you. It's an illness that can be treated and doesn't have to be a death sentence. I know because I used to be frequently depressed and wanted to die in my sleep. Today, I am grateful every day I wake up so that I can live another day.

Living with Alcoholism

The Diagnostic and Statistical Manual, the DSM 5 is current and provides symptoms and diagnoses for mental health and addiction problems and I encourage people to research this and learn about them. However, I will approach this chapter from more of an experiential angle than a diagnostic one.

I believe that there is both, psychological and physical dependence. Psychological dependence is developing thoughts and beliefs that include the word need. For example, I need to get high (drugs, alcohol or other) to cope, to get some relief . . . whether it be from feeling anxious, physical pain, emotional pain, anger and more. "Addictive Thinking" is common jargon. A common focus in treatment is the attempt to change this thinking. This is also why counseling and psychotherapy are so important.

Addiction progresses to physical dependence. Although narcotics are the focus these days due to the opioid epidemic locally and nationally. Withdrawal symptoms result from those physically addicted to opioids. It has been described as feeling like having the flu. Comparatively, withdrawal symptoms from alcohol are far more violent and potentially fatal. I say violent because those in withdrawal from alcohol can experience seizures, DTs (hallucinations) and even die.

Symptoms that are common with both opioid and alcohol withdrawal are: sweating, feeling hot and cold at the same time, muscle twitches, nausea, somatic complaints, sleep problems, irritability, depression and anxiety. This is physical dependence because the body depends on the chemical to function as a normal person. Clients often tell me that they don't know when they are high anymore. They describe it more like a stimulant and need it to get out of bed and go to work. This means that they depend on the drug to get out of bed. Hence, drug dependence.

Co-morbidity is a clinical term that refers to those with more than one diagnosis. This can include medical or mental health diagnoses in addition to the Substance Use Disorder or SUD. I, obviously, was co-morbid being that I had diagnoses of ADHD, Clinical Depression, PTSD and SUD in addition to Epilepsy. When comorbidity exists, it increases the complexities of the problems and therefore is more difficult to treat.

When I was 15 years old and in the Intensive Care Unit (ICU) and I regained consciousness, the first thing I thought was "Here we go again, the hospital. What else is new?" My head was pounding, I was dizzy, and the bed was soaking wet with my sweat because I was in withdrawal from alcohol. The doctor filled me in and told me that I was found passed out in some bushes and my blood/alcohol level was 0.5. I was naïve about blood levels or anything other than my Dilantin level which my mom had explained to me when I was six or seven years old.

I knew at that time, that the legal definition for a DWI or driving while intoxicated was charged when/if the blood level was 0.1 but has since been reduced to the current .08. This means that my blood/alcohol level was more than six times what was considered legally intoxicated. The doctor told me how lucky I was. That blood alcohol level frequently results in severe brain damage, retardation and even death.

I remained in the hospital throughout most of the detoxification process. I had tremors, was sweating profusely and couldn't sleep. I felt dizzy, weak and depressed. Every time my heart beat, my head pounded. I couldn't hear clearly either. It was as if I was wearing earmuffs, and the sounds were blunted. As usual, I was having seizures. It was strange for me to have seizures when I was drinking, because they usually occurred when I was in withdrawal.

After several days in the hospital, my mother told me that her mother (my Nunna) had passed away. I was going to be one of the pallbearers at the funeral. Seven days after I was put in the hospital and almost died, we were driving down to the state of Kentucky. I was still under the influence of alcohol withdrawal on the day of the funeral, and that was eight days after being hospitalized.

I hadn't had a drop of alcohol in the last eight days. I was wearing a three-piece suit on a hot and humid Kentucky summer day. I thought I was going to die, but I put on the best act possible. I was sweating buckets and felt like throwing up. The Kentucky heat, humidity and insects are bad enough when you are completely sober.

The emotional aspect was even worse. I was always depressed about life to begin with, but the death of my Nunna made it worse. I was also ashamed that I was living life as a drunk for three years already and couldn't even be sober while attending her funeral. That was not something a respectable grandson would do. To make it worse, as soon as the funeral was over, I was thinking about getting a drink to take away my physical and emotional misery.

As I consumed alcohol, it consumed me. It didn't take long for it to progress. Studying mental health and addiction in college helped explain things and put them in perspective. I had already experienced a lot of what I was studying, but my studies often confirmed a lot of what I already knew and managed to live through. The academics of things were foreign to me. It was interesting to learn about things academically and scientifically. I had the street smarts (or not so smart) and the hands-on experiences but not the book smarts.

I was like most, if not all, the people I have worked with in that addiction begins with the **use** of alcohol or marijuana. It frequently progresses to **abuse** and then to **dependence**. It can also progress in *what* is ingested (cocaine, heroin), and the *way* it is ingested/ administered, (progressing from sniffing it to smoking or shooting it, also known as intravenous. With alcohol, the progression could be from beer to wine to liquor with progression in the *strength* of the drug or alcohol. With drugs, one often begins with alcohol, then marijuana, then swallowing pills, to crushing and sniffing them, to sniffing heroin and on to shooting heroin.

I look back and that is just what happened. When I was twelve years old, I had consumed a quart of beer. I felt terrible and was dizzy and nauseous. I went straight upstairs to my bedroom to lie down, and it was like being on a merry-go-round. The bed was spinning, and I was getting sicker and sicker every second. I got up and ran toward the bathroom but didn't get there in time. I threw up in the hallway all over the wooden floor.

Some of it was in between the boards in the crevices, and I wasn't sure if I would be able to clean it all up. I was afraid that anything left would dry and stink. If my father didn't bust me now, he would bust me later. Being busted meant getting your ass kicked in my house. I was past the spanking or whipping with a belt phase. Between the dizziness, poor coordination and lack of balance, I wasn't sure that I could fake being sober if he saw me awake. I just said "To hell with it!" and took the chance that dad wouldn't find it when he got back from work and that was soon.

I was terrified of what he would do if he found out. I did my best to clean it up and hoped the Lieutenant of the Pittsburgh Police, my dad, would not be able to detect my crime. If he did, what would be my sentence? Would I get a tongue lashing? Would I be beaten with a belt, smacked in the mouth or worse? The tongue lashing was a definite.

The real question was would he hit me or beat me? Being beaten with the belt was a possibility, but that stopped being the standard form of discipline after I was nine years old. Being smacked in the mouth or punched was a real possibility. What wasn't a possibility was getting away with it or talking about it the next day when I had time to recuperate. Talking about things and using such times as a teaching moment did not happen in our household.

There was a chance of getting the belt, but the best chance was that I would get smacked or take a couple of body shots and be yelled at and threatened. He came home and yelled up the stairs to see if anyone was home, and I acted like I was sleeping. He tapped me and asked what was on the floor. He knew immediately that I had been drinking. It didn't take a cop to know this because I was hammered.

Strangely enough, he just told me that I looked drunk and that when I slept it off, he wanted me to remember how bad I felt at that moment and not drink anymore. Then he said, "Because next time, I will kick your ass." I knew I must be drunk because I couldn't believe what I was hearing. His first sentence sounded like he was trying to use this as a teachable moment, and this was quite foreign. The second sentence, threatening to "kick my ass if it happened again" was as familiar as the teachable moment was foreign.

To that point in my life, it was the first time I was ever intoxicated but not the first time I ever had liquor. The first time I had liquor was when I was six or seven years old. When my siblings and I were sick, we were given a half of a shot of whiskey as cough syrup. By the time I was eight or nine, dad had to take a pen and put a mark on the liquor bottles to make sure that we weren't drinking any of it behind his back.

As many other kids did, we would drink some of it and then add water until it was level with the pen mark on the bottle. My father was not a big drinker, so it was easy for him to bust us for watering down his whiskey. He may have been amused the first couple of times, but he eventually became very upset about it, so we stopped.

There was a lot of love in my home but there was a lot of hate, anger and fighting as well. Having a tongue that is as sharp as a razor is an understatement, and all of us had one. Though I was the youngest, I was not an innocent bystander. I was an active participant in us all trying to destroy each other. Verbal fights would escalate out-of-control, and physical fights would ensue.

I not only had the internal dialogue when beating myself up, but I had two older brothers, a father and grandmother who were also verbally abusive. This only reinforced what I had already believed. I believed that I was worthless, hopeless, helpless and pitiful. It all had to be true because the kids in school demonstrated that by the way they talked to me, and my family thought that too. They were supposed to love me and care about me, and they too were verbally abusive, so it must be true.

In addition to all the physical pain I had from the injuries suffered from seizures and being an active kid who had a lot of accidents, there was also the internal pain. Today I know the reason my drinking progressed is because I hated myself. How can I like, care about and respect myself if I am putting inordinate amounts of poison, aka alcohol, in my body every day, by the time I was fourteen years of age?

Think about the term detoxification. The short version is detox. Have you heard of the term, "detox center"? As in, "Did you hear that Jeff is detoxing again?" The prefix, "de" in Latin means down, down from or off to name a few. The "tox" is short for toxic. If you put the two together you have down from or off poison. I explain to my patients that when in withdrawal, he or she is emitting, seeping, draining, excreting, gushing or oozing poison from the body.

There is another diagnosis I had not mentioned and that is Oppositional Defiant Disorder (ODD). This is self-explanatory for the most part. This diagnosis is given to kids who do not listen to adults and particularly those in authority like parents, teachers and the police. I was so angry at my family and everyone else that out of spite, I would do the opposite of what was asked. Hence, the term, Oppositional Defiant Disorder. I guess it was my way of fighting back and showing them (those in authority) that they will not tell me what to do. It was also a way of making them as angry and miserable as they made me.

I was at Shuman Detention Center for the first of many times in the early-mid 1970s and into the late 1970s. I learned the hard way that the direction of my life was being guided by the choices I was making. Will you choose to hang with the partiers, the so called "cool kids" or those who go to school and do their homework? If the first two options don't work for you, there are the "jocks" or some other sub-group or subculture.

Peer pressure is a great force because we all want to be liked and accepted. The question is, to what length will we go to get that? Are you willing to compromise your morals and values to be liked and accepted and if so, have your really been accepted? When you are making unhealthy choices, at some point, you will pay for it! When you are making healthy choices, at some point, you will reap the benefits.

Making poor choices frequently results in negative consequences. You could get away with things that you are doing for a while, but the poor choices I was making landed me in juvenile institutions for seven years of my life. I continued to drink and make poor choices, and so I became an adult sitting in the Allegheny County Jail on several different occasions.

Keep in mind that your juvenile record will be kept private. But as an adult, it is a public record and anyone and everyone will have access to it. This means that when you apply for a job, the potential employer will see that you have a criminal record. This can hinder you and negatively influence an employer's choice to hire you.

Always remember that with every choice we make, there is a consequence. There are positive consequences, and there are negative consequences. Take control of your life and have the courage to change by making better choices. You will then welcome the consequences instead of dreading them. Changing my choices has renewed my life. Unfortunately, countless childhood friends did not change their choices, and they lost their lives because of it.

This explains why alcohol became so attractive to me from such an early age. The euphoria made me feel good. It also numbed the physical and emotional pain, at least while I was drunk. It made me not care about things. I was insistent that I didn't care and didn't realize until much later that if I didn't really care, I would not be as angry, upset and depressed as I always was. I also drank because I wasn't allowed, it was wrong, and it was illegal. This was my way of telling everyone in authority (especially my dad) to go to hell. For all these reasons, the more alcohol the better.

The more I drank, the better I felt and the less I felt. The more I drank, the less I remembered. I often had blackouts and a portion of my life was forgotten. Over the years I have heard others say that they stopped drinking due to having blackouts. They'd say that it was so scary to think that a portion of their day/life was forgotten. This meant that they had lost control and never wanted that to happen again.

The fact is, I never thought I had control of my life anyhow. With the way things were, I wanted to forget as much as possible. For all these reasons, blackouts did not scare me in the least. In fact, I welcomed blackouts. My goal every day and night was to become as close to comatose as possible by drinking as much alcohol and smoking as much marijuana as possible. My tolerance for alcohol increased quickly and subsequently, I had to drink more and more in order to reach that goal.

At age twelve, I was drinking three or four beers several times a week. That quickly grew to a six pack and then more. Before I knew it, I was introduced to Southern Comfort. I loved it because it was sweet and strong, almost like a cough syrup. It was way better though because the Southern Comfort got me drunk.

In my freshman year of high school, I was fourteen years old and consuming a pint of Southern Comfort during the ten minute walk from my home to my homeroom class. By the time I made it to my homeroom class, the bottle of liquor was empty. This might also explain why I cut school classes so much and the quality of my academics left much to be desired. By then, having ADHD was not my nemesis, but my abuse of alcohol was.

My dad would give me a few bucks a week for an allowance, and I would use a couple of quarters for the pinball machine at the pool hall. My pinball talents are not something I am modest about, but the truth is the truth. The song, *Pinball Wizard*, by the rock group, *The Who*, could have been written about me. Just kidding, but I was the best around.

I could do what is called "deaden" the ball on the flipper by keeping the flipper up and letting it down right when the ball contacted the flipper. Deadening the pinball slows the game a little so I could then use my marksmanship to pick off the needed targets and rack up the points.

I would build up to twenty wins and then sell them for a profit of three or four dollars. In no time, the buyer would lose those twenty games. I would put another quarter in only to win many more and then sell to the next person for another couple of dollars. At one point, the owner made ten the most games that you could win. Eventually, he took it down to five games were the most games that could be accumulated. That was my first experience with "downsizing" that decreased my income.

This is only one of the ways I made money for alcohol. I lived in Pittsburgh, Pennsylvania, so raking leaves and shoveling snow were two other ways that I made money to support my habit when I was a teenager. Spending time at the pool hall also helped me become a pretty good pool player. I used that talent to make some money too. It is not like I made a living doing one or all these things. I was penniless most of the time and when I had money, it was very limited.

That is why I began consuming Mad Dog 20/20. There was also Thunderbird, Wild Irish Rose and Night Train Express. For anyone who doesn't know, they are what we referred to as rotgut wine. They were all about 20% alcohol or 40 proof. By fifteen, I was an alcoholic and by sixteen or seventeen, I was a wino.

I began budgeting my money early on and never realized that the rotgut wine was how I was doing that. A half of a gallon was less than $2 at the time, and two quarts of beer were about the same price. So, with the wine I got literally more bang for my two bucks. After all, my goal was to become inebriated every day. This was a way to do it for the least amount of money possible. The sad part is that while I was doing the math to be efficient with my limited money for booze, friends were investing in their future and investing money in a home or an insurance policy.

When I was old enough to get served in the neighborhood, I learned another very efficient way to get drunk on a mere five dollars. At the time, a draft beer was fifty cents at a bar I frequented. Every day between five and seven o'clock, the draft beers were just twenty-five cents. That meant I could guzzle twenty draft beers in two hours for five dollars. If I had any money left over, I could go about eight doors up to the State Store, and get a fifth of liquor or a half gallon of the rotgut wine. My whole day had become centered on getting my beer, wine and liquor.

If I didn't do that, I would wait until later in the evening and use the money I had left to pay at the door for a party thrown by someone with kegs of beer and liquor. I remember, kind of, at times going outside and sticking my finger down my throat to make myself throw up so that I could go back in and drink more. I was a big marijuana smoker, and there was always someone lighting up a joint (marijuana cigarette) at these parties. I liked smoking it from a pipe (aka, bowl) and doing bong hits.

When I went to college, I was learning what all of this meant from a scientific, anatomical and psychological perspective. It explained what was happening to me, my mind and my body. My alcohol use progressed to abuse and then, dependence. For example, there are the terms, synergy and synergistic effect that mean: one plus one equals three or four. It means that when you drink a six pack and then smoke a joint, the one chemical "kicks in" the other. The euphoria/high is equivalent to drinking 9 or 10 beers.

It is very common that the clients I work with are mixing other drugs with their medication/s. Opioids, benzodiazepines, alcohol and barbiturates are all depressants. This means that they all depress or slow your respiratory system. However, overdoses often occur when heroin or methadone is mixed with benzodiazepines. Methadone is a synthetic opioid and was made so it has a longer half-life and remains in the system longer. It is used for pain management and to prevent withdrawal from opiates for these reasons. The synergy between the two drugs increases the risk of overdose and ultimately, death.

Some of our patients also drink and use heroin. Combining these depressants have a synergistic effect and can result in death. Because of my epilepsy, I took valium with my anticonvulsants when I was a kid. Thank goodness that I was taken off that medication before I got into my heavy drinking or I would have been history in my teen years. I was not aware of this until I began working in this field. Though I was a big drinker and experimented with other drugs over the years, I was never into pills and for that, I am grateful.

This information shone an even brighter light on how lucky I am to be alive. When I was in my early teen years, I was taking valium as an adjunct to my Dilantin to help control my seizures. I took a low dose of valium because I was young. I'm glad that it was removed from my medication regimen because by age thirteen or fourteen, I was drinking a lot of alcohol.

I was staggering home and having blackouts by the time I was fourteen or fifteen years old. I was lucky because if I continued to take valium, even at a low dose, my life would have been more at risk than it already was. It was also more likely that as I got older, I would require a higher dose and subsequently would be at a higher risk of harm. From that time forward, I only had to take valium or other benzodiazepines when hospitalized for detoxification.

Every morning for twenty years or more, I would wake up angry at the world. People have asked me why? I inferred that they were anticipating some long complex explanation when the simple answer was because I woke up. Well, maybe not that simple. After all, my sheets were drenched because I was sweating profusely most of the night while sleeping. A better description might be passed out.

I was having hot and cold sweats and shivering as if I was out in the winter weather without a coat. My head was throbbing and every time my heart beat, it felt like a screwdriver was being thrusted into my temple. My salty sweat was going into my open cuts and lacerations and was burning like hell.

I was shaking like a leaf from the DTs and had a severe case of dry mouth. It made me desperate for freezing cold water. My balance was still off, and I would carefully get to the Frigidaire and drink at least a quart of cold water in seconds. Whether it was liquor, beer or water, I always seemed to be guzzling something. I'd drink so much so fast and then would get a brain freeze as if my head was not hurting enough already.

When I got past that initial phase of daily hell I went on to the next phase. I'd get into the hot shower and clean my wound/s to prevent infection. The injuries I had from falls and fights would be soaped, rinsed and would be painful to different degrees depending on the severity of the wound.

When I got out of the shower, things were different. Despite the sweating before getting in the shower, the water still had to be hot. Therefore, when I got out of the shower, I felt a lot cooler and less uncomfortable because I had cleaned all the crud from my body, and my pores were open. However, the tremors became significantly worse, and I was shaking like a leaf.

My ears were ringing, and I couldn't think of anything other than getting some booze to take the edge off (stop the shaking and sweating). I was also in fear of having seizures that were more and more likely the longer I went through withdrawal before getting some relief. The more I thought about my pain and discomfort, the worse it seemed to get. At times, I would regain consciousness in even more pain after having one or more seizures because I wasn't able to find alcohol in time.

I remember more than once waking up with half my body in the shower and the other half on the bathroom floor. The plastic was broken where you stepped into the shower to enter. I had had a seizure and fallen. I was lying face down with my feet in the shower and my body on the bathroom floor, and blood was all over the floor. When I fell, I must have cut my shin on that broken piece of plastic. The flopping I did while seizing left blood all over the place. It took me several minutes to figure out what had just happened and longer to clean it up and stop the bleeding.

I would get out of the shower and dry my wounds that seemingly took so long to heal, and put ointment and bandages on them as best I could. Easier said than done with the tremors I was having. I got to a point where I didn't bandage them anymore and just let them air out. The wounds became like trophies received for being the biggest drunk and the biggest fool around. My father used to say that I swept up the sidewalk with my forehead and couldn't understand why I would do that.

Sports and music were my only two healthy outlets, both of which I did while I was high or while getting high. I tried to not be in a stupor until after I played ball. Playing sports was something that I was good at and was known for. I was usually one of the first few people chosen in a pickup game. Playing was euphoric for me.

I got a high by competing, by running up and down the court or striking someone out with my fastball or hitting a homerun or getting an interception in the neighborhood rivalry, "Turkey Bowl". Shooting pool games like 8-ball and 9-ball were other escapes, and I won a little drinking money doing that over the years.

All these activities helped me to escape reality while I was competing and most often winning. These were areas where I did have some pride and self-confidence. The reality was that my life was fun and games, but only when I was playing them. As soon as the games were over and reality set back in, my attention returned to drinking and smoking marijuana. I, occasionally, experimented with other drugs but those were my two drugs of choice.

My other addiction was smoking cigarettes and the more I drank the more I smoked. Gambling is another dangerous addiction to get into but was something I was able to do selectively. I only gambled when I was betting on me. I did not like betting on a horse or a number getting picked. I gambled with shooting pool, playing cards or one-on-one basketball.

I wanted to have something to say about the outcome, rather than just putting money up on someone or something and just hoping. I wanted my abilities and my quality of play to determine if I would win or lose. The other thing was that if I lost, I could blame myself and know that I lost because I was not good enough or I choked, not because I was unlucky or because someone else choked or blew it.

Drinking alcohol was a gamble too because I had an ability to drink a lot in a short period. I had a cast iron stomach and could mix beer, wine and liquor and seldom get sick. With alcohol abuse and dependence however, I lost every time. Believe me, it, in fact, is not a talent as my deranged mind once thought. On the contrary, it is something that will lead to your demise like any other disease if untreated or not erased from your life. Luckily, I never had enough money to become addicted to gambling, although with drugs, alcohol and my lifestyle, I was gambling with my life every day.

I was hospitalized many times at many different hospitals over the years for medical, mental health and addiction problems. My very first psychiatrist is a nationally and internationally known author and medical doctor/psychiatrist who is the founder of a treatment center in the area. The treatment center is a large facility with many different programs that treat adults and minors' addictions from the most intense level, detoxification, all the way down to the least restrictive level, outpatient treatment. He is a guru in the field of addiction.

When I met with him for the first time, I was sharing about how terrible and hopeless I was and the bad hand I was dealt from the start with my seizures, depression and ADHD. I talked about how those things made me depressed and suicidal. I blamed these things and my family situation for wanting to stay drunk. I was quite the broken record and repeated the *feel sorry for me* list of all the injustices that I had experienced in my first 13 years.

When I got done with my extensive list Dr. Schwartz stated, "I have some bad news, Mr. Parker. I don't have a magic wand to wave over your head and make everything better, and if I did, I would wave the wand over my own head." I thought he was the most heartless guy lacking in compassion and empathy. After all, here is a doctor who is sober and has a great life, and he is going to make a comment like that to a depressed, suicidal, alcoholic with epilepsy, ADHD and PTSD.

I had a few select words for him, and they were not nice. I told him that he is supposed to be this renowned psychiatrist who helps people, and this is the best he could come up with. I told him that he can go to hell and insisted on getting another psychiatrist. The next one would have to have more of a heart than he. I left steaming hot and told everyone that would listen about what happened with the big shot doctor.

Today, through a mature and sober view, I can see that he was trying to get me to understand that I will have to deal with reality at some point and not avoid it. I'd have to stop making an already bad situation worse by getting drunk almost daily to escape and avoid. Though I did not like him then, I chuckle at this experience, and I'm grateful to him for being real with me.

I'd like to think that some of the patients that disliked or even hated me over the years have come to realize that I was just trying to give them the truth. At least I didn't say some crap about a magic wand.

Today, I respect his opinion and have read a few of his books regarding recovery and spirituality. I also use some of his YouTube videos during counseling sessions with my own patients.

Post-Traumatic Stress Disorder

The National Alliance on Mental Illness (NAMI) defines Post Traumatic Stress Disorder as:

A) Intrusive memories (flashbacks or reliving the moment of trauma, bad dreams or scary thoughts),

B) Disassociation ("out of body experiences" or feeling that the world is not real or derealization),

C) Hypervigilance (being startled easily or feeling tense, trouble sleeping or sudden outbursts of anger), and

D) Avoidance (such as staying away from certain places or objects that remind one of the traumatic event. A person may also feel guilty, numb, worried, depressed or have trouble remembering the traumatic event.)

It is common for those suffering from PTSD to have comorbid mental health diagnoses like: Generalized Anxiety Disorder (GAD) Borderline Personality Disorder, OCD (Obsessive Compulsive Disorder) and/or Depression and Substance Use Disorder.

In the culture of addiction there is the expression, "war stories." It basically means that someone is sharing about their past experiences to impress, entertain or even brag about things they have done in the past. I want to make clear that this is by no means my intention.

The goal is to inform not to impress. The following is my history of various traumatic events that have contributed to many of my problems. I strive to show why I functioned so poorly and found alcohol my respite and even my best friend. I have experienced dissociation a handful of times, but the other symptoms have been a part of my life for many years.

In my drinking days, I lived a high-risk lifestyle. I often hung out and drank in dangerous neighborhoods. After all, I have lived in institutions, have been in jail and even lived in the projects for a few years. There were bars and cafés I frequented where the patrons could be friendly or dangerous. Most of the time there was not a problem but this time there was.

Collapsed Lung

(Shooting pool takes my breath away)

I went to a bar to drink, listen to music and shoot some pool. It was adjacent to the bar but considered part of the bar. On the left side was an entry to the real bar, where people went to drink. Next door there was also drinking but there was no bar. A half of a gallon of rotgut Thunderbird wine was wrapped in a paper bag and being passed around between a few of us.

There was a curtain and behind it was a table where a few more guys were playing cards for money. One of the guys asked me if I wanted to shoot some pool for five dollars a game. We had never met before and neither knew how good the other one was but we were both confident enough to play.

We played a few games, and each of us had victories and defeats. He was at his best by then, and I was just warming up and getting better every game. I would win a few games in a row and then he would win one. I thought that everything must be okay even though I was up about thirty dollars. After all, these guys were sharing their wine with me, and we were all drinking straight from the same bottle. I'd win a few more and then, he would win one. After about two hours of play I was up $100, and he was broke.

He then took the diamond ring he had off his finger and placed it on the pool table. He said, "I'm out of money, so I will play you for my diamond ring. If I win, I get my ring and the $100 back. If you win, you get the ring which is worth about $500." Keep in mind that this was the middle of the 1980s, so that was an expensive ring. It looked like it anyhow. I took him up on his offer. Five minutes later, I was in possession of his so called $500 ring, his one hundred dollars cash and the measly twenty dollars that I arrived there with.

I was excited and happy but tried not to show it. We shook hands, and I went on my way. I had the cash and my new diamond ring in my pocket and was not going to wear it until I was far away. I didn't want it to look like I was rubbing his nose in it. That could be dangerous to my health.

I couldn't have been more than a block away from the bar when I felt this piercing, burning pain in my side. When I turned and looked, it was the guy I had been shooting pool with. He had a coat rack in his hand and then dropped it. He apparently swung it at me like you would a bat and one of the hooks entered between my ribs and punctured my right lung.

As I fell to the ground, the assailant and his friend that watched us play pool were attacking me with punches and kicks to my face and head as I struggled for air. I could not breathe, but I still had the presence of mind to put both hands on my left pocket that was filled with what used to be his money and his ring. During all of this, I was thinking that they can kill me if they want, but they will not kill me and get the money and the ring back.

A couple of seconds, (which seemed like a lot longer) had passed, and I was no longer being hit. I looked up and had a blurred and limited view of them running west on Penn Avenue. I looked to the left and across the street where several people were screaming as they had witnessed the assault. It felt like my left eye was covered. I then realized that my eye was almost swollen shut. My nose was sore, and so was my head and the rest of my face. I guess I was still breathing but not much. I can't begin to explain the fear when I realized that I couldn't breathe.

As I got to my feet, people came over to ask me if I was okay. I couldn't answer them because my lung was collapsed. I knew this because my lung had collapsed before. I shook my head "no" and walked very slowly for a couple of blocks to a more residential area. I couldn't help but wonder if they would come back to finish me off. I was defenseless now because I couldn't breathe. I was enveloped in fear and knew I needed help.

A woman came to me and asked what happened to me. I couldn't answer because I couldn't breathe. I moved my lips to say "call the police or the paramedics". She called the paramedics and waited with me until they arrived. When they arrived, I looked at her and moved my lips to say "thank you". She was crying as she said, "You're welcome! I just hope you're okay." I smiled through the pain and said, "me too".

After the emergency room, where a tube was put in my side, I was taken to the Intensive Care Unit for a day or two. I was hospitalized for a week overall. I had a tube that went into my body in between my ribs not far from the puncture wound that occurred during the assault. The tube was to drain the fluid that had accumulated around my lung. This is a pneumothorax, whereas a hemothorax is a tube entered the same way but to drain blood rather than fluid. I've had both.

It was all terribly painful and ten times worse when I coughed, sneezed or when the tube was being pulled out. It was extra scary when they were pulling out the tube because the first time, my lung collapsed because the tube was removed too soon. When the tube was removed again, the lung re-collapsed. This time, as the tube was coming out little but little, a guy that doesn't fear much, was frightened. I couldn't breathe, I felt defenseless and hopeless, and I began to panic. I thought, "If I panic, how could I even hyperventilate if I need to?" I had reason to be scared. This time, the doctor waited long enough for the lung to mend, and the tube was removed without difficulty. It was nice to be able to breathe again.

The morning I was being discharged, I put the money and ring I had won in the pillowcase under my head until it was time to go. When the doctor said that I was discharged, I pulled the cash and ring out of my pillowcase. I got dressed to leave, counted the money I won and looked at my new ring before putting it on my finger. I smiled as I sat in the wheelchair and was pushed down the hall to the door with the EXIT sign above it.

Getting Kidnapped

(Hearse, ambulance or donut truck?)

I was kidnapped when I was 14 or 15 years old, and it affected me for a long time. Though it is illegal to hitchhike on major highways these days, at that time it was not. Thank God for that because I was still too young and having seizures, so I could not drive.

It was a fall evening and getting dark earlier every day. I was living in the suburbs with my mother at that time, but my heart and all my friends were in the city. I hitchhiked several times a week to go back home to drink and play sports with my friends and would return to the suburbs at night.

I was living with my mom about 20 miles outside of Pittsburgh. If I got lucky, it would only take one person to drive me close enough to home where I could walk the rest of the way. Other times, it would take three or even four different people to get home. Unfortunately, this was an evening that would require more than one ride.

The first one got me to a neighborhood just outside of the city limits. I was still about fifteen or sixteen miles from home. I was on Rt. #8 going north. This area had heavy traffic and a bunch of malls, stores and businesses. While hitchhiking, a vehicle passed me and then hit the brakes and came to a stop. It looked like a combination of a hearse, an old-style ambulance and the old bakery trucks. It had double doors in the back.

I ran to get in and smelled a strong odor of marijuana. There were four men in their early twenties with long hair. These hippie-looking guys said, "Hey man, where ya goin?" I told them that I was going about fifteen miles north on Rt. 8, and it would be cool if they could get me as close to Gibsonia, Pennsylvania as possible. They said to get in. Two of the guys were up in the front, and two were in the back with me.

The vehicle was laid out with wall-to-wall carpeting. It had purple lights built into the sides with a stereo system that was making my ears ring and my body vibrate. There was a cooler in the back filled with beer. They were listening to Led Zeppelin. I thought, "Wow, this is cool! Maybe they will give me a beer, and let me smoke some weed with them."

I've never been accused of being shy so I asked if I could have a beer. The guy up front passed the joint to the guy in the back. I waited for an answer and never got one. After they skipped me and passed the joint back up front to the driver, I got a weird feeling because they were very distant and aloof. They never answered about the beer, so I asked again. I assumed that they did not hear me because of the loud music. I asked a second time as the driver made a sudden turn off route #8. At the same time, a guy in the back answered, "No! Shut up!"

They proceeded down this back road that I'm sure they were familiar with, and I was not. Unlike the city, the roads were darker out there. It was pitch black, and I knew I had to make a move soon because the farther from the main road we got, the more danger I was in. "Was I overreacting or was this something to really be worried about? Were they just kidding me or trying to scare me? Were they going to kill me and dump my body in the woods?"

We were at least a mile off route #8 and with every second that passed, we were going deeper into the woods. It didn't make sense to me that they would make a friendly gesture to pick me up but then not even talk to me for the ten miles or so that we had traveled by then. "This couldn't be a joke, could it?"

I said, "Come on guys let me out". They just looked at each other and did not respond. It was time to make a move. I chose the front driver's side because the two guys up front had their backs to me, and the driver had to try and maintain control of the vehicle. I darted forward and jumped over the center console that divided the passenger and the driver. The two in the back and the passenger up front were trying to grab me as I kicked, punched and screamed at the top of my lungs.

While the driver made sure the car did not wreck, I was climbing over him and opening his door. As I got out the bottom of my pant leg got stuck. I felt pain at the heel of my foot. I believe my foot got cut from somewhere on the body of the vehicle, but to this day I don't know.

I ran into the heavily wooded area. I could hear their voices clearly, so they must have gotten out of the car to look for me, but it was pitch black out and just as I could not see them, they could not see me. I heard them say, "Let's find that son of a bitch." They quickly realized they were not going to find me and got back in the ambulance-like vehicle and drove off for fear that they would get caught.

I waited patiently until I heard a car approaching the area. I wanted to jump out and flag it down and get their attention so I could get out of there safely. "What if this was them again? What if they returned? Are they back to try and kill me?"

I didn't think I had a choice and so I tried to time it so that I would jump out onto this pitch-black road right when the car got there. "If it's not them, I could still be hit by the car. However, if I don't jump out in front of the car I am stuck in the woods and will have to walk a few miles to get back to the main road (Route #8)."

I didn't like the thought of that because of the injury to my foot. "They could come back at any time, and if I'm still on the road walking, and they could kill me!" All these thoughts and more were racing through my mind because of my ADHD. I was a mess.

I was about twenty yards or so from the asphalt road and saw the headlights getting brighter and brighter and bigger and bigger. I ran out as fast as I could, waving my arms wildly and screaming "Stop!" The car came to a screeching stop and beeped at me. That too, scared the hell out of me. I am out on this pitch-black dark road with gleaming lights coming toward me and this loud beep screamed through the air. I jerked as if I was having a seizure or had just touched an electric fence.

Once I realized that it was a car and not that black hearse or bakery truck-looking vehicle, I knew it wasn't them. I ran around to the side of the car and told the driver that I had been kidnapped and my foot was injured. I asked if he would please help me. Fortunately, he let me get in his car and drove me back to route 8 (civilization). He dropped me off at a gas station where the police and paramedics would come for the initial examination, followed by another trip to the hospital. I am forever grateful to that guy for stopping and taking me to safety. Whoever you are, and if you are reading this book, I thank you.

I gave the police the best description I could of the four men and of the vehicle. I was confident that they would be caught just because the car was so uncommon. The paramedics took my shoe off, and the sock was drenched in blood. I may have had some discomfort and stinging but I had forgotten about the injury to my foot until I was sure that I was safe.

To this day, I have no idea how I escaped from them. All I know is that it's amazing what a person can do when survival mode kicks in. For several months after being kidnapped, I called the police station to see if they ever caught my kidnappers and the answer was always no. I quit calling and many moons later, I am still a little bitter about them never being caught.

The two previous examples involved strangers but the situation I'm about to speak of involved someone I had been a real friend to. I thought he was a real friend, so what he did to me made it even more difficult to deal with.

The Louisville Slugger

(I thought he was my friend)

Brett and I had been friends for many years and partied and got drunk together all the time. I told my mother that he and I would be spending the whole day together, so she cooked a bunch of good food for us and dropped me off at his apartment before noon. By three or four o'clock in the afternoon, I was drunk. He wasn't quite as drunk as I, but I could tell he was getting there too.

We had been drinking liquor and beer and smoking weed together for about six hours when the party began to grow. By seven or eight o'clock, the crowd grew to about 20 people. I was blasted and my speech was slurred by then. Brett and his friends began to make fun of me and tease me because I was so drunk. The unusual thing about all of this is that I didn't know any of the people that showed up for the party. This was strange because Brett and I knew many of the same people and spent a lot of time together. I couldn't believe that someone who I had considered a good friend would be making fun of and teasing me because I was drunk instead of looking out for me as I would him.

I got angry about it and told him he and his friends were a bunch of asses, and I was out of there. I told him that it was obvious to me

49

that he was not a friend, and our friendship was over. I turned around and walked out of his apartment. I was ready to go anyhow because I was sloshed and could barely walk or talk. Seconds after I exited his apartment, I felt tremendous pain in my right kidney area.

At that same moment, my knees turned to jelly, and I buckled and fell to the ground. I looked up and Brett was standing over me with a bat fully stretched above his head. He swung the bat downward with full force. As the bat sped down toward my head, I curled up in a ball and covered my head with both hands. He repeatedly beat me on my head with the baseball bat with my hands slightly cushioning the blows.

After the fourth blow, he tried to move his hands to get a better grip on the bat. It was then that I grabbed his leg and bit it as hard as I could. At the same time, some of the partiers decided to grab him and hold him to stop further injury to my head and body.

I was pissed because this was a dirty move, and he wasn't even man enough to fist fight me. Yes, back in those days that's how we handled things instead of shooting each other which seems to be the norm today. I was also pissed that his friends allowed him to hit me four times with a baseball bat before choosing to intervene. I was particularly angry that while he and his friends were eating the great food my mom had made, they too had made fun of me and allowed him to pummel me with a bat.

While they held him, I stood up and slurred, "You are as low as it gets. You have a bat and still can't keep me down!" Even though I had just had the hell beat out of me I felt accomplished and energized just because I was able to get up and walk away from that. As I walked down the street, I relived what just happened in my head. I clenched my fists, gritted my teeth and screamed, "You can't stop me mother f***er!!!"

I was about two blocks away, and the adrenaline began to settle. Reality was setting in. As it did, the pain became more and more intense. I looked at my thumb, and it was three times its normal size. It had a big open wound and was bleeding. My head began to hurt more and more too. I felt around and noticed several big lumps and open wounds that were burning as well. I looked and my hand was soaked in blood. I knew that I needed stitches. I just didn't know how many. My head was soaked in blood, and I was sticky everywhere there was blood.

It became more and more difficult to even walk because the adrenaline was waning and going back to normal levels again. The longer I waited for my mother to show up, the more intense the pain was becoming. The pain in my back and kidney area was unbearable. I sat on the street curb in the dark, and tears from the pain came streaming. The salty tears melted some of the blood that had dried on my face. Some of the tears were from feeling betrayed by someone that I thought was my friend and that I had been good to.

I found the strength to stand back up and find the nearest payphone. I called my mother to tell her that she had to come get me and take me to the hospital. When we got to the hospital, she took pictures of my wounds. She had a Polaroid camera that would print the picture on the spot, and you could see the picture develop in seconds. She took a picture of my back, and there was a well pronounced bruise in the shape of the baseball bat. A picture was taken of my balloon-like thumb and the big laceration in it. The other pictures were not quite as clear because they were primarily images of my hair and blood. What was clear though was that I had lost a lot of blood.

When it was all over, I had about 40 stitches in my head. The thumb also required stitches but that would be done after they brought the swelling down. The Emergency Room doctor told me that from the first joint of my thumb to its tip, there were four fractures. That meant that there were four fractures within one inch. Brett had literally crushed my thumb when I used my arms and hands to cover my head. He had brutally beaten me with a baseball bat.

I sat in agony as I watched the Emergency Room doctor heat a straight pin with a lighter. I asked him what he was doing. He explained that he was sterilizing the pin before he stuck it in my thumbnail to make a hole. The hole would allow the blood to come out and would relieve the pressure and swelling. "I thought to myself, what the hell? I always hear about advances being made in medicine, and all the wonderful new things they are coming up with. A straight pin in my nail to relieve the pressure is the best they can come up with?" Well it worked, and though the crushed thumb healed as best possible, it still looks ugly today. There was no permanent damage to my kidney, but

I almost feel the pain I was having that night again as I describe that horrific day of my life.

I filed aggravated assault charges against Brett. He hired one of the top lawyers in the area with the money he made from allegedly selling drugs. He also used some of his friends, who were at the party, to testify against me. Despite all the pictures my mother had taken, he was acquitted. I was infuriated. The only satisfaction I got from the trial was that it probably cost him around $10,000 for his defense attorney.

Following the trial, a couple of people whom I choose to keep anonymous offered to hurt him badly or even kill him. If they would have offered this right after his acquittal, I'd like to think that I would still have declined the offer, but I honestly believe it would have been far more difficult to decline. I turned down the offer because I did not want either of them to be sitting in prison for the rest of their lives if I was selfish enough to take them up on their offer.

The closest I came to revenge happened when I saw Brett on the street a few months after the trial. My physical wounds may have healed, but the wounds beneath the surface were still open and painful. I was angry about what he did to me for years to come. We were on the same side of the street and walking toward one another. I recognized him before he did me. I considered attacking him at that moment but thought with my luck, he would get away with an aggravated assault, and I will go to jail for beating him up with my bare hands.

I had been smoking cigarettes for years and had bronchitis at the time. I had decided that the next best thing was to spit on him. It's been said that this is the lowest and most disrespectful thing that one can do to another. As he got closer, my heart rate went up and so did my anger. When we were close enough, I coughed up a bunch of phlegm that was yellow and disgusting. I spit it right in his face. I figured it was the least that I could do to pay him back. If I got lucky, maybe it would instigate a fight.

As the spit stuck to his face, I told him that I wanted to fight. I said that the advantage was mine because he had no friends with him, and he didn't have his baseball bat. The initial expression on his face was one of fury when he realized that someone had just spit in his face. The look quickly turned to one of fear when he realized that it was me who had done it. It was me who was standing just a few feet away from him. Brett turned down my offer and ran as fast as he could.

Brett moved out of the neighborhood soon after the trial. This was the first and last time I ever saw him. I would periodically, hear that he was hooked on heroin and crack cocaine. Supposedly, he was down to 150 pounds from the 190 pounds he was when we were friends. A decade had passed since that traumatic night, when I heard that Brett was dead from overdosing on heroin.

To this day, if there is a movie scene where someone is being beaten with an object, I cringe and turn away from the picture or change the channel.

The first three examples of traumatic experiences involved the perpetrators (them) and a victim (me).

A Metal Ladder is not Meant for a Tin Roof

(A roofer I'm not)

These next two incidents involve my stupidity as the culprit. My father had asked me to go up and caulk the roof for him. He said that he would be across the street with his binoculars directing me to the specific area he wanted me to caulk.

Dad went across the street and sat on the neighbor's wall as I climbed out the second story window and onto our porch roof. The ladder was on the ground and leaning up against the box gutter of the porch roof. I went out to the edge of the roof and lifted it up onto the porch roof. I then placed the ladder up against the hanging gutter of the third floor where he wanted me to caulk the roof. I was at least thirty feet from the ground.

The stupidity part was when I put the aluminum ladder on our tin porch roof. My father began to second guess himself and offered to come over and hold the ladder while I did the work on the top roof. I nonchalantly said, "No, I will be fine." After all, isn't that the typical response from a male teenager?

I climbed up the ladder and stepped onto the top roof. Dad directed me to "Go up and to the left a little." I'd go up and to the left a little and then caulk. I looked across the street and he lowered the binoculars and said, "Ok that's good." Before I was done, he would say, "Wait a minute. Just to be safe, go back up." He directed me to a different spot and said, "Caulk there too just to be safe." By the time he was satisfied, I had been off and on the ladder three or four times, and everything was fine.

I looked across the street, and he had taken the binoculars from his eyes and looked like he was ready to allow me to descend. I stepped down a couple of rungs and as my back faced him, I turned slightly, to look back and ask if he was sure. I didn't want to get off the ladder only to get back on it again. I didn't want to press my luck because in the back of my mind, I knew I shouldn't be up there on a tin roof with an aluminum ladder. As I turned back, the ladder began to slide out from underneath me and back toward the street. I thought, "Oh my God, this is it. I am done." It was like slow motion when the ladder continued to slide out from under me.

I literally rode the ladder down and out toward the gutter of the porch roof. I screamed as I fell. The ladder fell to the ground, and I was next. I was airborne for about fifteen feet before my chest hit the edge of the porch roof. The momentum of my body forced my legs to swing in toward the front of the house. I then fell another fifteen feet, and my back hit the ground. My head hit the ground immediately after. I was looking straight up at the sky, and it was a few seconds before I regained my scruples and realized what had just happened. The pain in my head was indescribable, and I was seeing stars in broad daylight on a sunny afternoon.

A ton of people must have heard me scream because even though I was partially concussed, I could see that there were a bunch of neighbors in a panic asking my father if they should call #911. I looked up, and dad was there to help me to my feet while rubbing my back and head. He said, "That won't be necessary. My kid is tough as hell. He'll be okay." He then took me to a restaurant and bought me a nice dinner.

I look back now and that seems negligent as hell, but dad was from the old school. Unless you were literally dying, you shook it off and moved on. So that's what I did. I had to literally shake for a while, before I was able to settle down and relax.

I had heard that when you have an accident your whole life flashes in front of you as you fall to the ground. I can attest to this, and assure you that it's true. I was nineteen years old at that time and every life experience I had to that point went through my head in the few seconds it took to fall thirty feet from dad's roof.

New Material for This Book

(Clumsy I Am)

The most recent of my many traumas occurred while writing this book. It was a Wednesday afternoon and getting close to the time when I would have to leave to pick my wife up from work. It was routine for me to take the garbage out at that time. Thursdays were pick-up days and when we got home, it would be dark during the fall and winter months. For eleven years, I have been dropping the heavy garbage bags over the railing. Then, dragging them across the yard before lifting them over my chain-locked fence for pick up the next morning.

When you come out of the kitchen door, a few feet to the right are 16 cement steps that go down to the cement walk and back yard. Our back porch was cluttered with boxes, and I was unable to toss the garbage bags over the railing without moving to the right. I was facing straight ahead and got closer and closer to the top step while continuing to toss each garbage bag over the railing. I was not paying attention and had moved too far to the right. I stepped off the top step while looking downward at the yard where I was dropping the garbage.

As I lost my balance, I began to do a cartwheel down the stairs. I reached out and grabbed the post with my left hand. The momentum of falling to the right made my body swing out toward the yard at which time the railing broke. I fell through it. It must have been terribly rusty. Wish I had known that, but it probably wouldn't have mattered.

I fell approximately twenty feet to the ground and landed on my right side. While airborne, my body flailed to the ground. I am a heavyweight, so I went down hard on the right side of my body. I knew as I was falling that it was going to be bad. I was in my mid-fifties and knew I would not get up as I had when I took a thirty-foot dive while helping my dad fix his roof. After all, I was about 35 years younger at that time and walked away from that one.

As I fell to the ground, I screamed "Help!" as loud as I could because I wasn't sure if I would be able to yell for help after I hit the ground. I landed with great force and the pain was indescribable. As you have read, I am no stranger to injury and pain, but this is up near the top of the list. The force was so great that the right side of my head smacked the ground too. My ribs were killing me, and I could hardly breathe. With every breath I took, there was excruciating pain. I thought, "My God, did I collapse my lung again?" The injury to my ribs was really bad. I always forget to mention that I broke my little toe on my right foot too. There was a terrible burning there but that was the least of my worries. That pain was drowned out by the pain of my ribs.

I tried to look around and see if help was coming. I moaned and groaned, and no one was there. It seemed like an hour, but it was only about five minutes before someone showed up to help. My wife was at work, but neighbors came to my rescue. A neighbor climbed over the fence so she could go into my house and get my keys. She unlocked the fence so the paramedics could enter my backyard.

I had fractured ribs 4, 5 and 6 from the front and the back while also breaking ribs 7, 8, 9 and 10. This means that seven ribs were broken/fractured in ten different places. Friends who have known me for a long time have said, "You don't do anything half-ass. Most people break one or two ribs, but you break seven."

The ICU/Trauma unit at a local hospital was excellent, and I was in good hands. The nurses were like angels flying in and out of my life of my room as I experienced intolerable pain. They were all so sweet and encouraging. They listened to our moaning, groaning, sobbing and more and brought some sense of comfort through all of it. To the trauma nurses at Mercy Hospital I say thank you for the mercy and the care you provided me with for the first couple of days.

When I was transferred to the regular unit, not so much. To make a bad situation worse, I was discharged from the hospital with an infected arm where my IV medication was administered. The nurse said that he was surprised I was being discharged when my arm was infected.

The homecare nurse stopped by my house the day after I was discharged and said that my arm was infected. She contacted my Primary Care Physician (PCP) after taking my vital signs and found that my temperature was 102.3 degrees. Fifteen hours after discharge, my wife was transporting me to the emergency room of different local hospital.

Within hours of my admission there, I was diagnosed with pneumonia followed by sepsis. My temperature reached a high of 103.4. I was being packed in ice to bring my temperature down. The doctors from the Infectious Disease Team were now ordering that I receive for four weeks, around the clock IV treatments of a strong antibiotic.

That wasn't bad enough. While trying to put a PICC line in my arm, the nurse struck a nerve located not far from my armpit. When she struck the nerve, I jumped, and every muscle clenched and tightened. Imagine that with seven ribs broken in ten places.

I had to be transferred from the hospital to a now needed long-term rehabilitation facility for the last three weeks of IV antibiotic treatment. I would also receive physical and occupational therapy to get my strength back after being in a hospital bed for five weeks before finally returning home.

The problem was that when I arrived, the antibiotic was not there. It had not been ordered. The severe pain, the narcotics I was taking and the many different things that had happened made this another of the many hospital visits. As usual though, I got through it with God's grace. For a little dark humor, I sometimes tell people that I feel sorry for Morris the cat because he only had nine lives.

Another of my many traumatic experiences occurred when I was in one of the many institutions I lived in for many of my childhood years. Due to my father being a Pittsburgh Police Officer, I was often targeted by others.

Blanket Party

(There is no party in blanket party)

One evening, three juvenile delinquents (as I too had been labeled) decided to give me a "blanket party". A "blanket party" is a vicious attack where the attackers wait until the person is asleep before they throw a blanket over the person's head and then attack them. They delivered countless punches to my head, face and body. By the time I removed the covers from my head and realized what had happened, everyone was back in bed. As I got up, I realized that the covers and sheets were covered in blood that was coming from my nose and lips. If that wasn't bad enough, the three perpetrators and many more were laughing and seemingly terribly amused.

Though I am not a paranoid person, I'm alert and careful today. I'm not in fear of being attacked, but maybe I should be. God knows it has happened enough to me. Just as a precaution, when I go out, I try to find the seat that will enable me to see what is going on. That is usually a seat against the wall so no one can come up behind me.

It seems that most people walk down the street with their headphones on and their attention on their cell phone as they cross the busy street blindly. I can't imagine doing such a thing because my past experiences will not allow me to be careless and put myself at risk.

When I am listening to music while walking down the street, I make sure that the volume is reasonably low. I will not cover both ears with my headphones. I always leave one ear uncovered so I can hear what is going on around me. I make sure to look behind me occasionally to see if anyone is approaching to assess the situation.

When I am facing a window, I use that window to see what is going on behind me. That window becomes my rearview mirror, like in a car. Some may find this to be paranoid in nature, but I know what people are capable of and just want to be as safe as possible. These experiences have shaped me to constantly have my antennas up. I have always been an observant person, but my traumatic experiences have taken my sense of awareness to a higher level.

I have occasional flashbacks, when I am in certain situations that trigger old memories. They take me back to those traumatic experiences. I can literally relive them. This occurred when I walked past Brett's old apartment where he had taken a baseball bat to me 25 years earlier. I stopped to look at the area where the assault had occurred. The event played out this time in my mind. I relived the bat coming down on my head and my face was grimacing, all my muscles tightened. I had said "Oh nooooo!" aloud before I realized it.

I still have trouble sleeping and have absolutely no fingernails. I chew them until I tear them out and they bleed. I must write with a pen because when I write with a pencil, I break the tip every time because I am so tightly wound. I press down on the tip with great force and don't realize it until the pencil tip breaks. I grip the pen so tightly that I get cramps and spasms in my hand.

A couple of times a year, I have nightmares of people kicking my head in or putting a gun in my face or of me falling from a roof. My wife has awakened me and told me that I was swearing and swinging. I was sweating and tears were coming down my face as I was reliving an old trauma.

My roles and responsibilities as an addiction specialist, social worker and psychotherapist has exposed me to people struggling with the same things I have, and some I still have.

Patients have arrived with injuries to the face and body and say that they were beaten and robbed. Another may tell of how he was jumped and pummeled when he was intoxicated the night before. I stay focused on that individual and remain objective while at work. When I go to sleep, similar experiences can be triggered, and there is an increased chance of me having nightmares.

This only happens a couple of times a year but that's enough for me. I have already been through it. It's a real pain that I must relive it again and again through the years. I'm grateful to have lived through my many traumas and even more grateful when I wake up and realize that it was just a dream.

I make sure to see my trauma therapist and/or take a couple of days off when needed. There is the expression in my field called "Taking a mental health day." The most important thing is that when this happens, I don't deny the seriousness of it. I get the help and support I need so I can remain clean, sober and competent at my job.

I am fortunate to be able to talk openly with my supervisor and administrators about such things, and it is not used against me. These experiences may have negative repercussions when I leave work as to sleep, flashbacks, etc. On the other hand, these experiences have been an advantage because they enable me to have insight about things that other clinicians may not have. Clients have told me more times than I can count that they are more willing to talk to me because, "You have been there." This is not to say that you must be screwed up or be a recovering addict to be an effective clinician. At least, not from my perspective.

No one is immune to trauma, and we can be exposed to it at any given time. I can assure you that those that live a high-risk lifestyle, as I did, are far more likely to be traumatized. The unfortunate thing about my PTSD is that it is still a part of my life. These terrible events (and many more I haven't shared) come back to haunt me periodically. However, I consider myself a lucky man because I am still here to talk about it. All I can say is that I feel sorry for Morris, the Cat, because he only had nine lives.

New Ways To Treat

Problems Identified in This Section

This section includes many different diagnoses I have had to deal with. Whether it is epilepsy, a learning disability, mental health problems or addiction, they all require some form of treatment. Some form of treatment is needed to minimize or eliminate symptoms so functioning and quality of life can be achieved and improved. Effective treatments can enable a person to live to their full potential and become more independent and productive.

The primary form of treatment for many illnesses, as you might guess, is pharmaceuticals. Let's face it, medication is used for epilepsy, mental illnesses and today, yes, addiction. The difference is that in the past there were far fewer choices of medications for epilepsy and mental health treatments.

To treat epilepsy, there are far more medications now to choose from. There are even combinations of food that can be weighed, put in a blender and eaten to treat seizure activity, depending on what kind of seizures a person may have. Certain kinds of seizure have been successful in treating epilepsy although there has been limited research. Call me cynical, but I believe that advocacy for research in this area is limited. If repeated and longitudinal studies were done here to show a high level of efficacy, far fewer pills would be sold, but that's just my opinion.

There is also what is called the Vagus Nerve Stimulator (VNS) that may have helped me had it been around many years ago. I say this because the Vagus Nerve Stimulator can be suggested for those that have the aura prior to a seizure. Please talk to your doctor about all possibilities in having your seizures treated. Research all the possible treatments, medications and supportive services based on what kind of insurance coverage you or your parent/s may have. Coverage or the lack thereof, can limit your choices.

There is also case management, counseling and family counseling. All can be helpful because epilepsy affects both the individual and the family in several ways.

For those with learning disabilities and particularly those with ADHD, there are newer and better assessment tools, support in the school systems and accommodations that are made today that were not available when I was in school. The answer, when I was in school, was that you were held back a year and considered badly behaved or mentally retarded (that was the term back then). In addition to getting tutoring and closer attention, there are medications like Ritalin and Adderall. In addition, there are things that can be done with the environment (smaller classes and one-to-one attention) and counseling to help those with this learning disability.

When it comes to mental illnesses, the most frequently used is psychopharmacology. Like epilepsy, there are many different medications available. A great deal of the newer medications do not have the severe side effects that came with the older medications like Haldol and Thorazine. In addition to medications, there are a lot of newer forms of psychotherapy that include Cognitive Behavioral Therapy (CBT), Dialectical Behavioral Therapy (DBT), Client Centered Therapy and Eye Movement Desensitization Reprocessing or EMDR. EMDR is one of the newer forms of therapy that are specifically for patients with Post Traumatic Stress Disorder.

When it comes to addiction, there are a lot of new techniques employed that include many forms of talk therapy like CBT and Client

Centered Therapy. A frequently used model of therapy for addiction is Motivational Interviewing. Methadone has been around for a long time, in comparison to some of the newer medicines. It was used as a last resort, but this does not seem to be the case anymore. Methadone treatment is specifically for opioid dependence and has become the *go-to* form of treatment since the mounting opioid epidemic came to be. It has been used for pain management for a long time.

There are newer medications that are being used for opioid dependency, and they are Suboxone and Vivitrol. Vivitrol is also being used for alcoholism when the only thing available in my years of addiction was Antabuse.

Whether it is for addiction or mental health, if a person is taking medication/s, I suggest that they talk to their doctor or doctors and consider counseling or psychotherapy in conjunction with pharmacological interventions for the best results.

I suggest that you research all your treatment options and then discuss it with your Primary Care Physician (PCP), your neurologist and family members. You may also want to get a second opinion before deciding what you want to do.

It always amazes me when friends, others and clients use hours of their day to research the best way to grow marijuana, to steal a car or start a meth lab, but won't research their anticonvulsant medication, the Vagus Nerve Stimulator (VNS) or the different models of psychotherapy.

I wish everyone the best, and hope that you find the right combination of medications, the right psychotherapist or any other form of treatment that will bring you and your loved ones the best results.

SECTION II

From Incorrigible to Institutionalized

From ages nine to seventeen, I spent seven of those eight years in juvenile detention centers and group homes that today, are referred to as RTFs or Residential Treatment Facilities. These are not the only kind of institutions at which I lived however.

There are hospitals. I have been a patient in every hospital in the City of Pittsburgh except Magee Women's Hospital. However, several years ago they began admitting men as patients. Today, it is just Magee Hospital, so of course, I have been there too. That means that I have been a patient in every medical hospital in the City of Pittsburgh, and there are many.

There are also psychiatric hospitals. I spent time in every one of these in the city at one time or another as well. After all, I had severe depression and was almost always depressed. Occasionally, I would become suicidal and would be admitted. Other times, I lost control of my anger and became violent and was 302ed more than once. Being 302ed means that you have been determined to be a danger to yourself and/or to someone else. It was an involuntary admission. The police would have to intervene, and instead of being arrested and taken to jail, I would be taken to the psychiatric hospital.

Now that I mention it, we cannot forget jail as being part of the institutional systems. I was a frequent flyer at the juvenile detention center. In fact, I made my first trip to the old juvenile court, as we called it then. About five trips were taken to the new one that is called Shuman Center. Sad to say, but the staff there knew me by name when I returned and would make comments like, "I've been expecting you" or "You decided to pay us another visit I see" or "What did you do this time?"

The detention center was usually the result of my poor responses to my problems such as running away, getting into fights at school, at home and in the neighborhood. I repeatedly ran away from home and eventually, refused to return home when the police picked me up. I was labeled an "incorrigible child." The term, *incorrigible,* is politically incorrect by today's standards, but back in the early 1970s, it was not. Quite simply, it meant that the child was out-of-control and could not be controlled or disciplined by the family and so required detention, structure and intervention/s from professionals. As a child, I was transferred from the Family System to the Child Welfare System, as it was called back then.

I certainly earned that label, but I was not the only person responsible for this. After all, I was physically, mentally and emotionally abused by my father. My mom was guilty of it too, in a far more subtle way. My parents got divorced when I was only two or three years old. The divorce was not a friendly one, and we, the kids, were exposed to a lot of hatred, resentment and hostility that they had for each other and freely expressed it to each other when we were around.

My father, literally, beat me and called me a loser. He told me that I would never amount to anything; that I was just a drunk and would never live up to my potential. He said that I didn't know how to listen and had no discipline.

The belt was usually to the rear end, but I remember having welts on my back and legs a few times because I ran from him, so he would be swinging the belt at a moving target. Dad would beat us with his leather belt until we were about nine years old. We were considered old enough to be smacked in the mouth or punched after that. The punches were usually body shots to the stomach or kidneys where we would fold over and/or fall to the ground.

Mom's abuse was far more subtle. She was a master at making a person feel guilty. A lot of it may not have even been considered outward abuse, but her ways took their toll over the years. At times, she could be very controlling in a different way than dad was. The other thing about mom was that she was never wrong. No matter what she said, it was the truth.

I certainly fit the profile of a troubled child. There were many more like me that were abused, unhappy and rebellious. There were even more that were in a worse situation and had more to deal with than I did. Based on my profile as incorrigible, disabilities like epilepsy, ADHD and my depression, Oppositional Defiant Disorder (ODD), smoking cigarettes and marijuana and drinking alcohol, I fit the mold. I had a lot in common with those with whom I was institutionalized. We were a group of troubled children that acted out and were rebellious.

The institutions I was placed in over the years, and some of my experiences while living there, will now be shared. The first real placement in a juvenile institution was McIntyre Shelter.

McIntyre Shelter was part of the Child Welfare System, today known as CYS, Children and Youth Services or CYF, Children, Youth and Families. It was run by the state of Pennsylvania. It was like a small campus with an administration building close to the highway, and farther inland, were eight cottages. Here we were the incorrigible, unwanted, abused and refugee children. We were to be rehabilitated, educated and eventually placed in foster care, adopted or returned to our biological families. When this did not happen, we were transferred to yet another institution, and then to another, until we were adults or we could go back home.

McIntyre Shelter is where I learned what a "hot foot" was. It was like an initiation ritual for the new kids that had been admitted. When the targeted victim would fall asleep, someone would put a match between his toes and then light it. Hence the term, hot foot. Naturally, the one committing the act and those watching thought it was hilarious. The one getting the hot foot, not so much. Quite frankly, I did not find it funny whether I was the witness or the victim. I never really liked "practical" jokes.

To me, there was nothing practical about them at all. I hate practical jokes because they often involve suddenly shocking or scaring a person. It wasn't funny to me from the start. Early on in life, I remember being frightened suddenly. The shock evoked a seizure. A moment of terror was followed by unconsciousness, and my body flailing all over the place.

When I regained consciousness, I was told I had a Grand Mal seizure (old terminology) or what is now referred to as a Tonic Clonic seizure, and that I was flopping on the floor violently. This was all because someone came up behind me and screamed "Boo!" in my ear.

There were only a select few kids that didn't get a hot foot. They were the big, mean, violent and intimidating kids that everyone was afraid of. People were too afraid of them to give them a hot foot. When word got out that my father was a police officer, I became a target. I was challenged by a lot of different kids because of this, but I held my own. When it was one on one, I could defend myself against any of the kids. There were always a couple who were tougher than I, so I was not picked on quite as much. When picked on, I would return the name, the elbow, a punch or anything else that was thrown at me.

I was "jumped" as it was called back then. This means that at least two and sometimes three or even four kids would attack me at once. I got the worst of those fights, but I made sure that I hurt at least one of them whether I had to punch them, bite them or kick them. My father always taught me to fight back. When I did, nine out of ten times, I would be left alone after that. He proved to be right about this most of the time.

I seemed to gain a lot of respect even from my enemies because I fought back. I think another reason was that I was a good athlete and very competitive. The fact is I hated to lose and would play my heart out and give it my entire effort. I think the more hateful kids respected me for the reasons above. I had a strong basketball game. I was very good at ping pong, and no matter where I went, I had the best arm. I could throw a baseball or softball farther and faster than anyone. I was good in the field, with my glove and could hit the ball a long way. Strangely enough, fighting and being a good athlete scored points with the tougher kids.

I felt for the not-so-tough kids. I also felt for the refugees that were there by no fault of their own. There were several Vietnamese kids there who fled with their parents to America during the Vietnam War. They were picked on a lot. I tried to protect and make friends with them.

There were two that I remember. They were brothers and like me, by nine years of age, were pretty darn good competition at ping pong. All three of us were about equal talent. Instead of gaining respect via fighting, we gained friendship through playing ping pong.

I can't remember her name now but there was an African American woman who worked there that was like a mother figure to us and was very sweet. I ran into her several years later when she worked at Shuman Center, and we embraced. I can't remember her name, but I thank God that she was there. She was one of the few positives that I remember about McIntyre Shelter. There were two other staff members that I can think of and they are Fred and Mr. McIntosh.

I had mixed feelings about Fred because he could be mean at times and at others, he was a pretty nice guy. He was one of those people I would begin to dislike and then, he'd do something nice. He loved listening to Johnny Cash's music. He was tall and thin and had wavy black hair. He dressed in the style of the late 1960s and early 1970s. He wore double-knit bell bottoms with a silk shirt with the top two or three buttons left unbuttoned. His black and gray-haired chest was exposed. He wore shades too, and the kids thought that he was cool. That is, until he got in one of his bad moods. I heard that he passed away many years ago, but I am not sure.

My memories of Mr. McIntosh are entirely different. He was a large man. He was only about 6 feet tall but weighed about 250 pounds despite his wooden/prosthetic leg. Not sure how or why he lost his leg, but I do remember that he was a mean person. Mr. McIntosh worked the night shift, and thank God for that. We only had to deal with him briefly until we fell asleep and briefly before we had breakfast in the morning.

We lived in large rooms that had several kids in each. It was not uncommon to hear clowning around or one kid making fun of another before everyone finally calmed down and went to sleep. It was referred to as horseplay.

One evening, the horseplay began and continued for a while. Mr. McIntosh yelled up the stairs, "All of you shut up or you will all see the consequences!" Just as things calmed down, I was able to fall asleep. Par for the course, I had a seizure, fell out of bed and landed on the cement floor that was covered with tile. The kids thought that this was funny and began to laugh.

Mr. McIntosh came in the room and thought that I had started the commotion and horseplay. This guy was about 250 pounds despite having a prosthetic wooden leg. He was a scary guy for a 9-year-old child who was not used to living in this type of environment. Though my dad was 250 pounds and physically abusive at times, he was my dad. There may have been abuse in my home, but it was my home and it was my father not a stranger who was the culprit. I tried to explain that I had a seizure and fell out of bed. I said that the laughter was just because they were heartless, and not from anything I had done to precipitate it.

He told me that I was lying and insisted that I come downstairs to his office to talk with him. He continued to confront and interrogate me about what just happened. I repeatedly told him that I had a seizure and fell out of bed. I tried to explain that I was exhausted, had a terrible headache and couldn't even think. He became angry because he didn't believe me. He was convinced that I caused the havoc upstairs and wouldn't admit to it. He got up from behind his desk, came over to my side and said, "Seizure? I'll give you a real seizure" and proceeded to grab me by the hair and bang my head off the desk three times.

The next day, I had lumps and bruises on my forehead. I cannot remember specifically if he was fired for that. I remember telling my dad what happened. By noon the next day, he was at the facility raising hell with the administrative staff. He was threatening to take care of the situation if they didn't. My father was a Lieutenant of the Pittsburgh Police at the time and probably had a few options in mind (legal and illegal) because he was infuriated. He told the administrators that he would have Mr. McIntosh arrested and McIntyre shelter would have a lawsuit against them if they didn't do something immediately about this. Dad also told me that he was going to confront Mr. McIntosh face-to-face and thought about beating his ass. This was not possible because his work shift was over, and he was gone for the day. Not sure what happened to Mr. McIntosh, but I don't remember seeing him after that.

I thought a lot about what he had done to me and hoped that one day he and I would cross paths again. I hoped it wouldn't be too soon because I wanted time to get older, bigger and stronger so that I could kick his ass. What he did to me would occasionally surface. When it did, I became angry and pictured myself taking his wooden leg off and beating him with it. In my head, I modified the tape that played of what happened.

Instead of being taken down to the office and being assaulted by him, I would picture myself punching him dead square in the mouth the first time he raised his voice to me, knocking his teeth out. His eyes rolled into the back of his head as mine did when I seized, and he would fall to the ground. As time went on and these kinds of scenarios were played out in my head, I would hope more and more as I got older, bigger and stronger that he and I would meet again.

The assault by Mr. McIntosh had a big influence on me. I tried to do the right thing when I first got to McIntyre Shelter. After being assaulted, I knew no matter where I was, I would not be treated fairly and, maybe would even be abused. I made up my mind that wherever I went I would make their life as miserable as they had made mine. I became very resistant to what was being asked of residents.

I ran away from McIntyre Shelter several times in the ten months I was there. Sometimes, I just left the grounds with another kid or two. We went across the highway to shoplift some cherry cigars to puff on. We thought it was cool, and they smelled and tasted good. Other times, I was far more serious about my escape and would be on the run for several days. This involved sliding down hills and jumping over fences to evade the police.

I would get away so I could sleep behind humongous garbage containers in back alleys located in downtown Pittsburgh. One of the times, there was a storm, and I was drenched. My feet were in my tennis shoes for so long that two or three days later my socks were still soaked. My feet were severely wrinkled as your hands would be if submerged in water for a long time. The wrinkles in my feet were very deep and looked like deep cracks were in them. My feet were red and looked like they were sunburned. The burning and stinging made it impossible to even walk, so running was not an option.

I eluded the cops and returned to my old neighborhood. I stopped by a neighbor's home because I was desperate for help. She was like a grandma to me. I often referred to her as my Jewish grandma. She adored me and I her. She took my shoes and socks off and gently washed and dried my feet before putting some medicated cream on them. I told her that I was tired of it all and just wished I was dead. She made me something to eat and filled my stomach before encouraging me to turn myself in so those that love me would not have to worry.

I did so but not for the reasons she suggested. By now, I had been away from McIntyre Shelter for close to a week and did not have my anti-seizure medication/s. I needed my medications because I had a couple of seizures while on the run. Whenever I ran away, I knew that my time was limited because I was going to run out of my medications and begin having seizures. I didn't care because when I made up my mind that it was time to go, I ran away from the facility.

The administration and clinical staff determined that I was not ready to go home because I frequently absconded, and for many other reasons. I was then transferred to "Bradley Home" that today is known as "Bradley Center."

Bradley Home was a Group Home when I was there. It is referred to as a Residential Treatment Facility or "RTF" these days. Bradley Home was a huge Victorian-style mansion. It was painted white and had two huge pillars on either side of the front door. It was large enough to house between ten and twenty kids and several live-in staff members. It was in the Oakmont, Pennsylvania area which was just outside of Pittsburgh.

The home was also very close to the Allegheny River and subsequently, the Hulton Bridge. We went to a local school, Riverview Elementary, where I set the record in the softball throw of one hundred and ninety-one feet. I got to attend the US Open at the Oakmont Country Club in 1972 because I was in the Little League baseball league. We, the players, were used to pick up trash during the event.

I remember a staff member at Bradley Home who I will call David. He played the electric guitar and formed a band with us, the residents. I played the tambourine and sang back up. Those memories bring a smile to my face but there are also memories that I am not so fond of.

The fact is I continued to struggle with my seizures, my anger and violent outbursts. I ran away from there frequently. Even though I was only ten and eleven years old while there, my depression and suicidal tendencies were getting worse. When I ran away, I would go up on the bridge and look down at the water of the Allegheny River. I would imagine myself falling and hitting the water violently and going under. I would picture my body floating and being taken from the river by first responders. I would see them zipping up the body bag and declaring me dead like you see in the movies.

I began to lift my leg over the railing of the Hulton Bridge in an attempt to make my suicide a reality. Thoughts like "You can never do anything right. With your luck you will screw this up and be in a damn wheelchair the rest of your life". "Remember this is final. Once you jump, there is no turning back. You can't reverse your decision and any chance you have of a better life later will be gone." "Think about how much you have put mom through already. This would destroy her if after all her efforts you killed yourself."

Then there were other thoughts like "It sure would take a miracle with the damn life I am living. It's not even worth sticking around. Why? So that I can be in institutions and jail all my life? So, I can be picked on and fight and beat people up and be mad and drink and get high the rest of my life? With the seizures, I will never drive a car. No girl is ever going to want me. Dad is going to keep beating me up, and telling me I am a piece of shit."

The internal battles were non-stop when I was in this state of mind which was quite often. I had happy and enjoyable moments occasionally, but they seemed to be the exception. I was mad that I couldn't jump off the bridge and wished I would just die in my sleep. I did not want to go on in my situation, my circumstances.

Bradley Home was like anywhere else in the behavioral health profession and had a lot of turnover. After all, I alone could be enough for burnout and reason to leave, but there were 10-20 of us there. As many in the profession know, the pay is not good either. There are many reasons for turnover, and this place was no different. There are specific things about Bradley Home that I liked. It wasn't as bad as some other places I would later be, but it was common for staff to become burned out, fired or just leave.

Bradley Center hired a new staff member that seemed like a nice guy at first. It all turned out to be a lie. I would soon find out that he had an ulterior motive. It did not take long for him to show that he was not there to help us. He was a predator. I can attest to this because I became someone he would focus on shortly after he began working there.

A characteristic of a child molester can be and often is patience. They take the time to groom their victims. Grooming is a term used to describe a process in which the predator develops a friendly relationship. They do things to gain your trust, and try to form a bond with his/her victims. He/She invites you to their house to watch sports or a movie. They might offer you beer, candy or marijuana to gain your trust. What appear to be friendly acts are all a hoax. They are calculated behaviors. Their goal is to sexually victimize the child.

It was not uncommon for a staff member to pull a kid aside to speak with them about an inappropriate behavior or comment made. When this new staff member pulled me aside to speak with me, something just didn't feel right, and I was suspicious. Even at the young age of ten, I was analytical and alert. My mom and dad had taught me to be aware of and in tune with the things that were happening around me. She wanted me to be in tune with what happened before, during and after my seizures. My dad taught me to be alert for my own safety. Being a cop made him aware of what people are capable of. Whether it be these reasons or just a gut feeling, I knew something wasn't right about this guy.

One afternoon he called me away from the crowd and said that he wanted to talk with me. He was staff and hadn't done anything wrong to me to this point, so I walked over to him. He asked me to sit down. I can't remember the conversation but in the middle of it, he began to talk more softly so that I could barely hear him. I now know that this was because he wanted an excuse to move closer to me and he did.

In the middle of the conversation he grabbed me by the back of my head and pulled me toward him. He then tried to give me a tonsillectomy with his tongue. I turned my head to the side as quick as possible but still ended up with his saliva on the side of my face. I gave him a knee to his crotch and ran to the building as fast as I could. I immediately reported him to Mr. Eddie Holden, CEO. Eddie had someone sit with me in his office to console me while he investigated what had just happened. This staff member was fired. Another abusive act had been committed against me.

This was the second institution I had been in, and two abusive acts had been committed against me. I began to think that these places were worse than home and the abuse I was trying to escape. At least at home, it was a family member abusing me and not a stranger. At least it is physical abuse and not sexual abuse. From this experience, I learned to trust my own instincts and judgment.

Ironically, I would later work with the sex offender population. I saw many of the same traits and characteristics in patients that I saw in the staff member that preyed upon me. My biggest challenge in working with this population was to remain objective. I remember a child psychologist that was mandated by the criminal justice system to receive therapy for molesting several children in his private practice. I was the group facilitator, and he was one of several patients attending. I had to make a conscious effort to remain objective and professional and this was very good training for me to learn how to do that.

The best thing that could have ever happened to me at Bradley Home and in my life was meeting the CEO, Mr. Eddie Holden. I say this for many reasons. To begin with, he was one of the few staff that really meant it when the workers in the child welfare system would say that their primary goal was to do what was in the child's best interest. With many, that was a bunch of hot air. With Eddie, he demonstrated that every day.

In fact, Mr. Holden became a personal and a family friend as I got older and grew from a troubled child to a troubled adult. He was always someone I could call when I needed someone to talk to. Mr. Holden and I got together periodically to break bread and keep each other up-to-date on what was going on in our lives.

By today's standards, Mr. Holden would be considered unethical because he had a personal relationship with a former client. Our friendship lasted into my late forties when he passed away and left a beautiful wife and children behind. His legacy is that he touched many, many lives while he was here. He helped me to believe in myself. He attended all three of my graduations from community college and the University of Pittsburgh where I earned my Bachelor's and Master's Degrees. Eddie is also the reason that I am happily married today. He encouraged me to go on-line and try eHarmony.

If anyone else had suggested that, I doubt that I would have followed through. It was Eddie though, and I knew he had my best interests at heart. He had proved that time and time again over our thirty-five years relationship. Thanks to Mr. Holden, I met a special woman and within seven weeks, we were engaged. Within nine months, we owned a house and were married.

Several years after being discharged, the Bradley Home relocated. I am not sure if it was true, but I was told that they relocated because it was in a high risk area for kids. This is because it was close to the river and the bridge. There was fear that a child could jump from the bridge, get hurt on the shore or fall in the water and drown. When I heard the explanation, it hit very close to home. My experience on the Hulton Bridge flooded my mind. I had to shake it off and get back to the present time. I lived at the Bradley Home for 13 months before being transferred to St. Francis Hospital due to my ongoing seizures and severe depression.

St. Francis Hospital no longer exists but was in the City of Pittsburgh for nearly a century. Wow! Does that make me feel old. I was admitted to St. Francis for the first time when I was just twelve years old. The hospital had a section for medical care and another for psychiatric care. I'm sure I was there for medical reasons at least once. My memories about St. Francis are from the several times I was there for my dual diagnosis of clinical depression, out-of-control behaviors and alcohol abuse. I say abuse because I was in the early stages, had just started drinking but was not yet addicted

My first admission there was probably the longest and that was for about 90 days. I look back today and what an irony that the world-renowned Dr. Schwartz was the first psychiatrist I ever had. He is a Hasidic Rabbi, a Medical Doctor and author of approximately 60 books. He is the founder of a treatment center in 1972, with its main facility in Aliquippa, PA just outside of Pittsburgh.

I remember our first encounter and quite simply didn't like him. I was the typical hard-nosed kid who could not understand how this "old man" with a beard down to his belt buckle, a medical degree, a bunch of money and fame and with seemingly no problems, could have any idea of what I was going through. I was convinced that he could not help me. I thought, "If you want to help me, give me a twenty-dollar bill, and let me the hell out of this mad house so I can buy a little weed and a case of beer."

That was far from what happened. My memory of our meeting is very limited. What I do remember is that Dr. Schwartz was a straight shooter and was not someone who beat around the bush. He was not mean or loud but quite the contrary. He spoke softly and got straight to the point.

I told him my story about the abuse at home, all the suspensions from school for fighting because I was picked on, made fun of and my seizures. I told him about my ADHD and all the academic struggles that come with it. I'm sure that I also told him about the abuse from the staff member at McIntyre Shelter where I was assaulted, and the staff member at Bradley Home who tried to molest me. I went on for about fifteen minutes with very few breaths in between. I then waited for a response from him, for words of wisdom and this is what I got.

In his soft tone he said, "Well Jeff I have some bad news." I was waiting to hear something about my treatment that I wasn't going to like, and he said, "I do not have a wand to waive over your head to make everything better, and even if I did, I would waive it over my own head." I thought well if I had a wand, I would beat this guy with it, and then wave it over my head. I was so angry, but that was probably because this was not the response I wanted. He was giving me a reality check.

I was hoping that he would tell me that there was a magic pill that would take me out of my misery. Strangely enough, this conversation took place nearly 45 years ago and I have never forgotten it. It has stuck with me over the years. I was angry about it for a long time. However, my interpretation of his message changed when I did. I came to find that I only have one mother who would tolerate me and have unconditional love. This is the real world and if there is some special thing that could be done to change everything, I'm going to have to do it for myself. If you want something another person has, go out and earn it just as they did. I think that he was relating to the internal things like serenity, contentment and happiness as much as the monetary gains.

I think about that experience quite often. Today I interpret his message to promote motivation rather than sitting around getting high and feeling sorry for myself. I see this quite frequently in clients

I work with today and share my experience with Dr. Schwartz. I also see the same anger and frustration in them toward me that I had for him. I hope that years later, it may have an impact on them because it certainly did with me. Today, I have a plaque hanging on the wall in my office that carries a similar message. It reads, "Life is not a remote so get up and change it yourself." My thanks go out to Dr. Schwartz for the meaningful but not so pleasant memory. I must admit that today, it brings a smile to my face. In a nutshell, today I use Rabbi Schwartz's seemingly heartless remark to remind me that it is time to quit feeling sorry for myself and get off my buttocks and do something to change it. By the way, I wasn't crazy about the new psychiatrist either, but I would be a therapist and work with him 26 years later. How is that for an example of how hard work can pay off and feeling sorry for yourself will keep you stuck.

I was not pleased with Dr. Schwartz, and my parents were not pleased with the hospital because St. Francis was where I began smoking cigarettes. The hospital required that parents give consent for their child to smoke. There was no way that they would allow their twelve-year-old child to smoke. By chance, I became friends with a girl who was smoking and willingly gave me cigarettes after teaching me how to inhale.

My father may have had me inhale a cigar after catching me puffing on a cigarette when I was nine years old, but I had never inhaled a cigarette. I think that big fat stogie may have been weaker than the cigarette because she smoked non-filtered, Chesterfield cigarettes.

I was gagging so badly. She was laughing as hard as I was gagging. That might have been part of the incentive for her giving me cigarettes at the start. She got a kick out of seeing me struggle. My throat would be so sore, and I would have a headache. The room stopped spinning after the second or third one, but it took a while before my throat could handle the Chesterfields. After about 3-4 weeks, I thought I was a pro. I had the smoke coming out of my nose and everything.

In everyday life, St. Francis was like all the other institutions in that it was very structured. There was a schedule to follow every day. I remember waking up with a hangover from the medications that they were giving me. Shortly after, we'd go downstairs to the cafeteria and stand in single file. I think the cafeteria was in the basement where we would get the nutritious food that was plopped on the plate. In all fairness I don't remember if the food there was good or not, I just know that institutional food usually isn't.

Patients were given their psychotropic medication/s followed by the psychotherapy part of the day. What I remember most was the "quiet hour" every afternoon. I remember it because I hated it! Don't forget that I have ADHD and could not sit still back then. I had to stay in my room every day, for a nap or just to be quiet hence, quiet hour. The other thing I hated was being locked in my room for that hour because it seemed like days. The worst thing about the quiet is that when quiet and alone, there is only one thing to do and that is to think.

All I could think of were the negative things because I couldn't see any positives in being depressed and suicidal while locked up in a mental hospital. I'd think, call me cynical if you want but you take my life and my current situation and see if you can find any positive things in it. If you do, you are the nut not me. As you can tell, I spent a lot of time feeling sorry for myself and that is not a good trait for someone with severe depression.

Today, I tell my depressed patients and those with racing thoughts that when they think a lot, their depression is guaranteed to get worse. It is crucial that the depressed person fight it and get with other people and not stay alone. It's just as important that they get busy and try to get their mind focused on something other than the problems they are having. At that time my depression was severe, and I spent a great deal of time thinking about suicide and ways that I could die.

Much of that hour was spent thinking about falling from the window of the hospital or intentionally walking out in front of a speeding car. Other times, I would ruminate about something that was said to me that was hurtful or ignorant. I would become angry and think about hurting that person. I would play back mean things that my father had said to me or the staff member who tried to molest me. I thought about what I would do to them if I was big and strong enough to beat them to a pulp. I would picture myself going through the unit of the hospital and destroying everything! Throwing and breaking chairs and tables.

Quiet hour might have been quiet on the outside, but on the inside, there was a war going on. To me, quiet hour meant it was time to endure an internal battle with no interruptions unless it was one of the few times that I fell asleep. Almost always that hour was one of violence, confusion, racing thoughts, rage, sadness, a lack of hope and thoughts that I was worthless, lonely, a loser and nothing was ever going to change.

That explains the quiet hour. There was also a room known as the "quiet room." Saint Francis himself must have had a fetish for quiet but I certainly didn't. I hated quiet. I also hated the quiet room. It was just another term for seclusion or isolation. When the staff determined that you were out-of-control or at risk of harming yourself or someone else, you would be secluded from others and placed in the quiet room.

Back then, you could be subdued by security while a psychiatric nurse shot you in the hip or buttocks with some type of sedative like Valium or Thorazine. It was near the end of the straitjacket era, but I remember being put in one at least once. I am certain that I was sedated with the shot in my butt several times and put in restraints as well.

The shot was just what you would imagine. It was a big long needle that would often leave a bruise and soreness at the injection site for at least a day or so. While several staff members would hold me down, the psychiatric nurse would inject the medication.

Once the medication began to take effect, the staff that held me down would then get up from on top of me and back away. After they saw that the medication was taking effect, they would carry me to the quiet room. There were anywhere from two to four people that carried me, depending on how sedated I was and how easy it was for them to grab my limbs and carry me to the quiet room. The time spent there was usually two hours. At that time, (depending on the dose they gave), I would awaken and be groggy and still somewhat sedated.

The quiet room was padded with mats on the floor and walls so that those who banged their heads or punched and kicked the walls and floor could not harm themselves. The rooms had these humongous windows and heavy-duty screens that were locked with a skeleton key. This was so the windows could be opened in the warmer months and the screens locked so that no one could jump to their death, as I had imagined countless times.

If there was one thing I hated, it was being locked up. I remember begging staff members to leave the door open a couple of inches, and I would cooperate and not get crazy. Well, they'd tell me that was against policy and then lock the door. Soon after I heard the door lock, I would snap. For some reason, instead of punching the padded walls or floor, I would punch the window screens countless times, nonstop, until all my energy had been spent.

When I stopped, the skin and blood from my knuckles would be embedded in the screen. I usually gave staff hell because it was easier to stay in there while unconscious or at least sedated. Though no one wants to be locked up or confined, I figured out years later why it was so difficult for me. I remembered that my parents used rope and cord to wrap around my crib because I had severe seizures and was an escape artist.

My mother explained that it wasn't just the rope and the cord. After they had put a fence up in the backyard, there were extra pieces. She explained that they put the extra fence on top of my crib and then used rope and cord to secure the fence on top of the crib to prevent me from escaping when they were busy or sleeping.

Unfortunately, St. Francis was just one of the psychiatric hospitals I was in during my journey. The others include Western Psychiatric Institute and Clinic and Woodville State Hospital.

Woodville State Hospital--I was admitted to Woodville at the young age of thirteen. With it being a State Hospital, Woodville was long-term, and I was there for more than a year. There were a few other state hospitals in Pennsylvania, and they were Torrance, Mayview and Dixmont State Hospitals. Patients at a state hospital could be there for many months to many years. Being admitted to Woodville, at the age of thirteen, was a scary experience, at least in the beginning.

To give perspective on how times have changed, the state hospital era in Pennsylvania ended many years ago. There are very few patients in a state hospital, and it is said to be for the criminally insane. Very few patients live there. Only Torrance is the closest to Pittsburgh since the closing of Woodville. This means that very dangerous, unstable, mentally ill people are the only patients that are admitted and stay there.

It's also true that up until the late 1960s and early 1970s, homosexuality was a mental health diagnosis. People with epilepsy were often placed in state hospitals for many years because they were considered incapable of stabilizing and were possessed with evil forces. I was very young, had epilepsy and was having Grand Mal seizures on a regular basis. Had I been aware of these things back then, I would have been even more frightened.

You may have seen the documentary that Geraldo Rivera did on Willowbrook State School and if not, I suggest that you find it and watch it. It will give you perspective on how people with mental illness were treated back then at that facility and many others. I highly recommend that readers Google it and watch the film. It shows extreme neglect, abuse and how deplorable the facility and its living conditions were. Though the conditions at Woodville were by no means as bad as Willowbrook, there were hints of neglect and the warehousing of patients. But the conditions were clean and far from deplorable.

My biggest complaint about Woodville State Hospital was the 400 mgs a day of Thorazine that was prescribed to me by the psychiatrist. Many patients were heavily sedated. Despite my young age, I knew that this was a form of controlling us, and I resented it. I showed this every time I had an opportunity.

When patients' families were there to visit, I would hear the doctor saying how good the patient was doing, and I couldn't help but interject. I would tell family members that if they look closely, they will see that they are not doing well but are being made into a zombie with the psychiatric medication/s they are taking. I'd go on to tell them that we couldn't even think for ourselves. We were all being sedated by the medication, and it was that simple. To the defense of the clinical staff however, the psychiatric medications at that time were far more limited. There were fewer choices, and the medication back then had far more side effects.

Even 400 mgs of Thorazine every day couldn't slow me down. Once I got up in the morning, regained consciousness, shook off the cobwebs and had breakfast, I was off to the races. Every morning I got up, I felt like I had a hangover. I remember waking up with my head throbbing to the beat of my heart. The headaches would last for the first hour or so but would get better over time. I guess I developed a tolerance to that as I had alcohol.

I did not do the "Thorazine shuffle" like many other patients did. For those who don't know, the "Thorazine shuffle" is a term meant to be humorous while describing how a person looks while on Thorazine. The "Thorazine shuffle" to me is best described as if a person is sleepwalking while in a trance or a robot walking in slow motion. They would also have a blank stare that made it seem like they were in their own world.

I already struggled with concentration, comprehension and memory due to my Attention Deficit Disorder, but the grogginess from the Thorazine made it even more difficult. The Thorazine may have calmed the hyperactivity but exacerbated the cognitive deficits already present.

The other thing I hated was afternoon nap time. We were asked to stay in our room for one hour every day. "What the hell was it with these places", I would think. "I don't need a damn nap. I need to go out and exert some energy. I need to play sports, run around, anything but lie down for an hour." Like all the other institutions, structure and routine were key components. These components were well needed and helpful in many ways, but didn't fit with a hyperactive thirteen-year-old kid.

The most calming and therapeutic treatment that I remember while at Woodville, was not the psychotropic medications or talk therapy, but the walks the staff took us on through the countless acres of farmland. I remember an orchard where there were limitless trees and apples. I was told that many years before I had arrived, patients took care of the land we were walking on.

There were seats and benches at various places. I would see old folk sitting there with a blank look on their face. I wasn't sure if they even knew their whereabouts, and this made me sad. I would sit with them and talk to them. I would hold their hand or shake their hand as I introduced myself.

Sometimes the blank look continued and there was minimal to no response. Other times, I would get a smile. There were also times when their eyes or facial expression would show a hint that they were still cognizant of what was going on. I wondered where their family members were. Did they have anyone that genuinely cared about them? When was the last time someone came to see them? Did they have any children or grandchildren?

My thoughts eventually went back to focusing on me. I'd think, hell, I am not in any better shape than they are. I'm on medications and have seizures and can't think straight. I'm an out-of-control nut who is in a state hospital before I am even old enough for high school. Sometimes I envied those who didn't know where they were or what was going on because they didn't know how bad their life sucked and I did. I may not remember specific people or their faces, but I remember that a couple of people I introduced myself to would see me days later and smile or wave at me. Though that sounds like a small thing, it was big to me because that meant they remembered me due to a kind and humane gesture I made by showing an interest in them and that's all most of us wanted.

There were periodic activities that included indoor and outdoor sports, playing cards, softball and throwing the football. The walks gave me a sense of peace, temporarily at least. These activities were a positive way to vent and expend energy while doing things that I enjoyed. Being outside and doing these things were a break from the yelling and screaming I often heard due to outbursts of anger and hallucinations that patients were having.

My memories of Woodville State Hospital are limited. I do know that if someone heard you were at Woodville, they assumed you were long gone from reality, and there wasn't much hope. Just like the stigma I see today with the addicted population, and particularly patients at a methadone clinic, the stigma and stereotyping are alive and well toward those with mental illness. The bottom line is that we all want someone to care about us. We are all human beings and need help at one time or another. Take the time to reach out to someone and get to know them before you judge them or assume things that are not in evidence.

In addition to St. Francis and Woodville, I frequented another psychiatric hospital known as Western Psychiatric Institute and Clinic (WPIC). Like St. Francis, and unlike Woodville, WPIC was a local, short-term hospital where I was admitted both voluntarily and involuntarily. Sometimes I signed myself in for admission. Other times, the police brought me there because I was out-of-control and probably needed to go there but was not willing to do so without a fight (verbal and physical).

Western Psychiatric Institute and Clinic--WPIC was at least honest about the title of "the quiet room". They referred to it as solitary confinement and that it was. I hated nap time there just as I had at the other psychiatric hospitals at which I stayed. WPIC was even worse though because they did not have the activities that the other hospitals had. They did not have the gymnasium or a swimming pool like St. Francis did. At least, I don't remember them having any such thing. I did play as much ping pong as they would allow, and one of my competitors was the psychiatrist.

My times at WPIC occurred when I got a little older and was in my late teens and early twenties. I had several visits there after drinking heavily and intentionally overdosing on my medications. Other times, I was admitted for threatening to kill myself or for episodes of rage and was determined to be a danger to myself and/or others. Hurting myself was usually the reason for being admitted. I believe one of the admissions was for becoming violent with my father.

I had attempted suicide several times over the years. It could involve anywhere from 50-180 pills of my anticonvulsant medication, Dilantin, depending on how new or old my prescription was. At the time, I was taking six pills a day. A full prescription was a quantity of 180 pills. Another factor was my age. When I was a youngster, I would take 20-30 pills, but as I got older, I would take more. On more than one occasion, I remember being asked by medical staff to drink this charcoal-looking stuff that would help me to throw up the pills I had taken. I hated it because it tasted terrible, and because it was defeating my purpose.

I recall another time when, as usual, I finally had enough of this life. "To hell with this world. I'm not taking a measly 50 or 100 pills." I only had a couple of days left of medication before I ran out and would soon be getting a refill. I decided to wait until I got my new prescription. The couple of days I had waited was more time to ruminate and become even more angry, depressed and suicidal.

I took the new bottle out of the bag and looked at it. The bottle was filled to the brim with 180 Dilantin, 100 mgs pills. I took one handful after another of pills and washed them down with a liter of Nikolai Vodka. A short time later, the bottle of pills and the bottle of alcohol were empty. In about thirty minutes, I was unconscious. Right before passing out, I remember thinking, "That should do it this time".

My mother said that she had tried calling me at my apartment several times and did not get an answer. Mom had a sixth sense. She told me she knew something was seriously wrong and rushed from her place to mine. When she arrived at my apartment, she saw me unconscious but still breathing. She said to save me great embarrassment, she cleaned my apartment for the 15-20 minutes it took paramedics to get there.

When the paramedics arrived, they put a device on my leg and pumped it so that the pressure would send blood rushing to my heart and my head. I was then taken to the Emergency Room. Once cleared medically, I was admitted to WPIC. Prior to being admitted, the patient is taken to "the deck." It's just a nickname for the place where the clinical intake information is collected prior to being admitted.

I'm sure it happened more than once, but I remember a time when I was admitted involuntarily which is referred to as being 302ed, in the state of Pennsylvania. I was taken to what was called "the deck" where the admission process was to occur. Well, I decided I was not going to be admitted without a fight. I became violent, and it took at least four security guards to take me to the ground and subdue me. One of them was "Slim" who I knew when he was a guard at Shuman Detention Center when I was a kid. His nickname was "Slim" because he was anything but. He was about 6 feet 3 inches tall and weighed well over 300 lbs.

After being taken to the ground, "Slim" talked to me and calmed me down. He had me promise to calm down, and they would let me up without being sedated. Out of respect for "Slim", I kept my promise and was admitted without any further problems. I saw him years later and thanked him for being good to me both at Shuman and at WPIC. Despite the bad memories with institutions, there were good memories like this, from meeting some good people who really cared.

I believe it was at WPIC that I learned the details of ElectroConvulsive Therapy (ECT). I was there the first and only time I was put in a straitjacket. I have already described the emotional struggles there. Every time I was locked up, I was put in isolation, but this caused my anger to be as bad or worse. In the late 1970s or early 1980s, I was put in a straitjacket. The straitjacket and ElectroConvulsive Therapy, better known as ECT or shock therapy, was used less and less around the country (so I heard), but ECT was still being used at the local psychiatric hospitals in Pittsburgh, including St. Francis and WPIC.

I remember another time that I could not control my temper and had my typical episode of rage. I can't remember what precipitated it, but I was always on edge and could lose it at any second. I picked up tables and chairs and was throwing them. Security had the area evacuated of all patients and most staff. There were a couple of clinicians that tried to help me de-escalate while a code was being announced over the intercom. This let security know that there was an emergency and their help was needed. I never tried to hurt any of the staff over the years, but I always tried to resist and fend them off for as long as I could. I don't remember if I ever threw punches or tried to assault staff or security.

After bobbing and weaving, pushing furniture their way and running to another area to buy time, I always ended up cornered. There were always more of them than me. I would push them or wrestle them. I'd resist when they grabbed my limbs, but I never tried to hurt them. Just the same, they never tried to hurt me, but we all would be a little scuffed up. There was a lot of wrestling and headlocks. Sometimes a little blood was spilled, but it was almost always mine and was incidental rather than intentional.

The four and maybe as many as six security guards eventually gained control of me. The psychiatric nurse shot me in the buttocks with a sedative. When enraged, I can't be sure how many people or security guards were there, but I know it was at least four. They stepped back as the drug took effect. When I regained consciousness, I could not move. I was still groggy from the sedative they injected. My arms were wrapped across each other as if I was hugging myself. My left arm was across my body and tied behind the right side of my back. My right arm was across my body and tied behind the left side of my back. I had been put in a straitjacket.

The difference between a straitjacket and a regular jacket is that the sleeves are significantly longer on the straitjacket so they can be tied behind your back with no slack. It's also much more stylish than a regular sport jacket or blazer. Seriously, my arms were completely restricted, and there was no chance to move either of my arms.

There was another time when I had been placed on a carrier where I could be transported from one place to another. There were leather straps wrapped around my ankles and wrists. I was tied to the bars of the carrier, restricting me from any movement of my legs and arms. These were situations that literally drove me crazy. Restrictions of any kind do not mesh well with someone that is angry, hyperactive and has seizures. Whether it is locked in, locked up or my body being tied down, restrictions and I have never been a good match.

The other extreme intervention used at WPIC was ElectroConvulsive Therapy (ECT). Most know it as "shock therapy." Not sure what the laws are these days, but back then, parents had to give consent for the treatment to happen if the patient was a minor. The patient would have to approve it, if they were an adult. Unlike the sedative injection, ECT could not be ordered by a doctor or a nurse because they thought a person was out-of-control and needed it. I never had ECT and thank God that my parents never approved it. As an adult, I sure as hell wouldn't approve it.

With ECT, a seizure/convulsion is induced, and God knows I didn't need that. Like many different treatments, there are success stories and nightmare stories. I heard a couple of success stories for ECT but far more nightmares. This is similar to psychotropic medications where one person will tell you how much a medication has helped turn their life around while the same medication not only didn't help but turned one's life into a horror story with side effects and/or out-of-control behaviors.

Regardless of the outcomes, many considered ECT barbaric and out of touch with time. However, many psychiatrists still believe in ECT. I believe that it is still used in some places but usually as a last resort. When all else failed, it would be time for ECT. To my understanding, ECT is a procedure, if you want to call it that. The patient has electrodes that are temporarily attached to the head. It is turned on, and it induces a convulsion or seizure.

Multiple sessions of ECT can be ordered. A successful intervention is when the multiple sessions of ECT are completed and horrible memories, that were the cause of their depression, have been eliminated. The risk is that the person walks around like a zombie until they come out of what seems like a trance. I remember seeing patients return from ECT and feeling so bad for them.

They appeared hopeless and disoriented, much like those of us that were prescribed Thorazine. A blank stare was very common in the mental hospitals. It could be both a sad and scary thing to see. Due to my age and naivety in the beginning, the blank stare was scary. Before long, I had seen it so many times that it no longer scared me, but it made me feel sorry for that person. Every time a patient returned from ECT treatment, I would think, "I hope this is worth it to them and they get something good from it, but they aren't doing that shit to me".

After being exposed to the life inside of psychiatric hospitals, I often wondered why these places didn't have better security. I don't mean on the units of the hospital, but at the entrances. Anyone could walk into the hospital right off the street. I knew how much I resented these places for locking me up and controlling my life, but I also knew it was needed. After all, I was an out-of-control kid and young adult who had a lot of anger. Most of it was self-hate. I didn't have it in me to commit a mass murder, but I know there are people out there who are more than capable of it.

Unfortunately, on March 8, 2012, Western Psychiatric Institute and Clinic made national news when a 30 years old, former patient, named John Schick, walked into the lobby of WPIC and began shooting, killing two and injuring seven. Since this tragedy, there have been significant changes to security at the facility.

What bothered me most about the incident was that there are middle schools and high schools in the Pittsburgh area that had metal detectors and security at the entrances of our schools before they were at WPIC. I am not saying that all the mental health patients are dangerous by any means, but there are outliers like John Schick, and preventative measures could have been taken earlier. If they had, this nightmare may never have occurred.

It was surreal to see that a place I had frequented in my younger years, as a patient, was under attack by a former patient. My heart goes out to the victims, their families and friends that were injured and killed on that terrible day.

WPIC was part of my earlier life, and years later, it would be part of my life again. Though I have not been a patient there since the old days, I had several semesters of training within the WPIC system when I had practicums and internships there while at the University of Pittsburgh. My internship was not in the hospital, but in a couple of different WPIC outpatient programs.

Patients that I work with today are often hospitalized for co-occurring disorders, and my personal experiences with psychiatric hospitals and institutions provides insight many others don't have. I know that someone can be out-of-control, angry, depressed and suicidal and still have a good heart. I know that someone can lose control and hurt someone else and feel bad about it. I know the many assumptions that are made when someone is admitted to a mental hospital. I know, because I've lived it, around it and through it.

Then there were the legal places that I had frequented including Shuman Detention Center.

Shuman Center is a juvenile detention center located in Pittsburgh, Pennsylvania and serves children and families in the Allegheny County area. Like WPIC, it is not a place that I could put in chronological order because I had frequented it so much. I was at the original Juvenile Court in the Oakland neighborhood of Pittsburgh just before it shut down, so when I went to Shuman Center it was brand new and state of the art.

I was probably ten or eleven the first and only time I was detained at the facility in Oakland. In December of 1974, Shuman Center was opened. I am sure that I was one of their first detainees. I was born in 1962, so my first time there was when I was twelve years old. There are no exact dates or specific reasons for being incarcerated, so I will summarize.

Prior to being admitted to Shuman Detention Center, I was likely at Woodville State Hospital or the Home for Crippled Children. Today, it is known as The Children's Institute. More than likely, I had run away or gotten picked up for public intoxication, fighting or something similar. Shuman is located on top of a hill as many things are in Pittsburgh. It consists of several huge buildings that are connected and that house hundreds of troubled youth. The building spans a large piece of property, looking almost like a campus but not quite.

When you approach from the outside, you can see a nice baseball and softball field. To prevent escape, the fenced in field has barbed wire with razors that are in a circle atop the fence, making it nearly impossible to escape without being cut up. I remember rare occasions when someone would use their shirt to throw over the barbed wire in an attempt to get over the fence with as little injury as possible. Most did not make it. Those that did were picked up shortly after and would need medical attention because they had injuries from the barbed wire and razors.

I was very athletic when I was a kid and wanted to be free as much as anyone else but no thanks. I was not going to climb that fence and get cut up trying to get over the barbed wire. I'd just wait until I got to the next institution and run from there. That was my mentality.

Shuman Detention Center had security guards to greet you at the entrance. You were frisked every time you went from point A to point B. Administrators' offices were to the left in a designated area separate from the living quarters. Past the entrance were the guts of the building. There was a large open area that was used for visitation and court hearings. There were three juvenile court judges that included Judge Jackson, Judge Nelson and Judge Tambelli.

Judge Jackson was an African American fellow who was a decorated military man who did not cut much slack for any of those that found themselves in his courtroom. White and black kids alike that had him for their judge would say, "Judge Jackson is not prejudiced, he sends everybody away." I never had him, and thank goodness for that. There was even word that he was even tougher on the African American kids because he wanted them to have higher expectations of themselves. He seemed to think that giving them tough consequences now could prevent bigger consequences in their adult years. Not sure if that is true, but this is what I heard when I was detained at Shuman Center.

I had Judge Tambelli and was in his courtroom several times. I was not aware, until I was writing this section of the book, that he had passed in March of 2018. Judge Tambelli had also served in the military. His obituary said that he had been a Supreme Court Justice for the state of Pennsylvania for many years before retiring. Judge Tambelli was fair but stern. When he said something, he meant it. As much as I wanted to dislike him, I didn't because he was a man of character and played by the book. I couldn't blame him for that because he was fair and that's what was important to me.

When there were mitigating circumstances and room for his discretion, he would give kids a chance. If they blew it, they could depend on facing more serious consequences next time. His obituary also said that he was an advocate for children. I believe that to be true despite decisions made that were not favorable for me at the time. He would explain why he made the decision, and I was getting what I deserved. Most importantly, he seemed to genuinely care.

I heard over the years, that he moved up from the juvenile and family courts and was a state Supreme Court Justice. I was working in downtown Pittsburgh as a psychotherapist after earning my Master's Degree in the field of Social Work and heard that he frequented a specific restaurant at lunch. I was not sure if he would be there or if I would even recognize him if he was there. I walked in anyhow hoping to see him. I knew that he was an attractive Italian guy with dark hair that was probably gray by now. He was always well dressed in a beautiful, expensive suit and tie.

I walked into the restaurant and looked around. I heard a large group of people talking and laughing, and I gazed to my right. As I looked closer at those sitting at the table, I saw a handsome looking man that seemed to stand out from all the others. I told myself to take a chance and asked if he was Judge Tambelli. He said, "Yes I am. How can I help you?" I apologized for the interruption and then asked if I could speak to him privately, and he kindly obliged.

We stepped out into the waiting area and I explained who I was. I introduced myself and he said, "I remember you Jeff! Your dad was a Lieutenant with the Pittsburgh Police, right?" I confirmed that he was. He then asked how life has been since those days. I told him that my struggles continued for many years after my Shuman Center years. I explained that today, I was clean and sober. I added that I managed to earn a Master's degree from Pitt and was working as a psychotherapist.

He shook my right hand with his and grabbed my forearm with his other hand and said how happy he was to hear that. He said that he remembered that I had a lot of problems and was so glad that I had made it through those years and was doing good things with my life. I wasn't sure what it meant to him one way or another, but I needed him to know that I had always respected him and the decisions he had made when I was in his court. This conversation was almost thirty years since I had seen him, and he remembered me and my father. This confirmed what I already knew, that he was a good man that cared.

Before the court proceeding back then, you had to try and settle in and adapt to the living arrangements that were so much like jail. Because we were minors, they called it detention rather than jail or incarceration. I loved that one. We were locked up and frisked every time we went somewhere. When we returned, we were even strip searched after family visits. Everything was scheduled at a certain time. The food was terrible, and though we were jailed, they called it detained.

The various units we lived in were back and away from this open area to minimize disturbances for visitors and court hearings. I can't recall exactly how many units there were, from seven to ten units, and I was in almost every one of them throughout my tenure there.

Downstairs was the school where all of us were to have class and study just like anywhere else. The problem was that we were all at different levels academically so there was no real curriculum to go by. In addition, we could be there one day and gone the next. The usual stay was a few weeks to a few months, so even what would be considered a long stay would not be more than a semester of class. There was little to no continuity with my schooling, and I would pay for it later.

There were observation cameras everywhere. Security staff had posts in different sections of the building and the units we lived on. These posts were little rooms with cameras, switches and buttons everywhere. Each one was like its own control center. Security had walkie talkies to communicate with one another. Announcements were being made frequently over the intercom.

Whenever we went from point A to point B we went in single file. When we arrived at our destination, each of us was searched from head to toe to make sure that no one possessed drugs, cigarettes or weapons. Security would see on camera that a door needed to be entered and would press a button. The door would then be opened. When you entered the unit, on the left was a "smoke room", also called a "snack room."

When you put a lot of kids that have been rejected from their family and society in the same unit, conflicts and fights are inevitable. There were bullies in the unit as there were anywhere else but even more so here.

There were kids who did not take showers who would literally smell. I remember the staff asking a couple of the bigger kids in the unit, including me, to put this smelly kid in the shower. While fully clothed, the staff member would give us a scrub brush and soap. Some held him down while others applied the soap and shampoo. Then it was time to use the scrub brush until he decided to improve his hygiene.

I remember another kid who had the worst breath and didn't brush his teeth too often. He would be asked to breathe on the locks of the doors to melt them so that we could escape. There were so many cliques, and a lot of making fun of and bullying going on. We were damaged and disturbed already, and the way you were treated here by your peers was a powerful force against anything positive that the staff, therapists and teachers were trying to do.

I remember an extreme case when we were given chocolate milk and cookies as an evening snack. A certain kid was targeted. Before being given his chocolate milk, two kids had urinated in it. It didn't seem like anyone was immune except for those that were known to be dangerous. Some were there on very serious charges like aggravated assault, attempted murder or sexual assault. Of course, these were usually the bullies. There were other kids involved with gang activity.

Back then, kids were rarely tried as adults. This has changed significantly because many juveniles that have committed violent acts are incarcerated in a unit in the Allegheny County Jail. The unit is separate from the adults, while also being separate from the juveniles at Shuman Center. They are considered too dangerous to be detained there.

Detained or not, my escape was sports. Shuman was brand new and had a great gymnasium and basketball court. I loved going to the gym to play ball. This was where I was respected because I knew how to score and rebound. I was always one of the better players. On the other hand, I had a target on my back when word got around that my father was a Lieutenant of the Pittsburgh Police force. I had to keep an eye out for dirty shots like elbows or tripping, and make sure to return the favor. In most cases, it was important for me to return the favor or they would keep doing it. If this meant getting into a fight, then so be it.

There was also a ping pong table on the unit. The more time I spent in Shuman Detention Center, the better I got at ping pong. I had a reputation for being a really good player and was tough to beat. Whenever new kids would come to the unit and talk about how good they played ping pong, others would tell him, "If you think you're that good, go play Parker." My serve was one of my strengths because just like the several different pitches I threw, I had many different serves. I put different spins on all of them. One serve was like a fastball, another like a changeup, and the other was like a curveball.

In fact, I had practiced for hours until I mastered a serve from the snack room to the ping pong table that was about 25-30 feet away. I am left-handed and would throw the ball up high and when at its peak, the ball was struck hard, and I twisted my wrist at the same time. The ping pong ball would travel to the other end of the detention unit. The spin would make it curve through the air and hit my side of the table, bounce over the net, and land on to the opponent's side.

I was successful six or more times out of every ten attempts. The only problem was that when the person returned the serve, I couldn't run to the other end of the unit in time to keep the volley going and would lose the point. For that reason, it was just a show-off kind of thing and can't be used in a game if I wanted to win.

Shuman Detention Center might have been a new place when I was there, but it became old quickly for me because I would be back again, again and again. The thing I probably remember most is that we all had very small rooms that were just like a cell. We would be locked in there every night. It was just like jail because it took a while for the kids to settle and quiet down so others could sleep.

Being locked in a tiny room, having seizures, and living with kids that might be more accurately referred to as young criminals, is why Shuman was not one of my favorite places.

The Home for Crippled Children is another of the many institutions I lived in.

The Home for Crippled Children--Today this same facility is called The Children's Institute. It's located across the street from The Tree of Life Synagogue where the mass murder occurred on October 27th of 2018. I lived there for eight months. While recollecting the process and chronology of my institutional life, I am beginning to see how old I am. This is another facility that was almost brand new when I was admitted there. This was a place that housed children with different physical, mental and developmental disabilities and impairments.

The disabilities could include things like paraplegia and quadriplegia, those like me with epilepsy and the sight and hearing impaired. In fact, I was taught the basics of sign language while I was there. I still remember the alphabet. I even remember the signs for doctor, nurse, fire, a boy and a girl. I even learned the sign for bullshit. Of course, as a kid, you had to know at least one swear word. Though one of the purposes of this book is to educate, I will keep this sign to myself.

Having a disability contributes to and creates many other problems. It affects family members and caregivers. The disabled person is dependent on others to transport them places. We are treated differently which affects and/or limits our social life. Subsequently, many that lived there were angry, confused and depressed. We had many behavioral and academic problems as well. There were teachers, counselors, physical therapists (PTs), occupational therapists (OTs), speech therapists and many paraprofessionals there to help all of us in whatever way they could.

I remember a kid my age that had lost both hands and had two stumps. Like me, he was angry at the world and began smoking at a young age. He would hold the cigarette to his mouth with his stumps and to freak people out, he would put the cigarette out with his stump. He explained that they were numb, and he didn't feel a thing as he snuffed out the lit cigarette.

Another young man was a normal size from his waist up, but the lower portion of his body (his legs and feet) were the size of a young child. He had holes in his back that had been covered by surgery, but you could still see the deep indentations. I truly admired him because he would not allow anyone to help him and was self-sufficient.

I will refer to him as R. Well, R was on a carrier for most of the day. He would be on his stomach while pushing himself from one wall to the other wall and traveling down the hall. He would grab the door with one hand and hold it open while forcing himself through the door with his other. He surprised me because he shot pool pretty well. Like the rest of us, R had a temper and could be mean if he was in a bad mood. Only then, did I stay away from him. Otherwise, he was a guy I admired because of his determination.

One of my favorite memories of The Home for Crippled Children was the relationship I had with a worker I'll call Rich. He was an African American man who was always encouraging and had a big, beautiful smile that was contagious. He had some gray hairs and a well-manicured goatee. When I teased him about having gray hair, he would give me that big smile and respond with, "There might be a little snow on the roof, but there's still a lot of fire in the furnace." As a kid I thought that was the coolest comeback.

I also thought Rich was a special guy because his job was to make various tools and equipment to accommodate a child's disability. He had his own shop that was on the lower floor. He would measure the height, length and width of a kid's wheelchair to make seat cushions that would raise a person up and/or make them more comfortable. He also had projects to do in the building that would make it more accommodating for the population being served there. This could be doing something like improving a prosthetic device and making it easier to use or more efficient.

I knew it took not only a talented person, but a caring and feeling person to do that kind of work. I have always been an observant person. I could plainly see the joy it brought him when his project was successful. He would be pleased at making a child happy and more hopeful. He was pleased that their future would be just a little easier than it was before he made the device. He was also a very patient person.

If it wasn't quite what they needed he would go back to the shop and adapt or modify until he perfected it. This is why everyone loved Rich. I visited him at The Rehabilitation Institute for twenty years after I left until he retired. Wherever you are Rich (I know your real name), you made a difference in a lot of children's lives, and I love you for it.

I have a lifelong friend that nicknamed me "went and did it". I was always getting into things and was not the best behaved. While at this facility, I had my cut-up crew. We would sneak off the unit, and I would use the plastic ID card we were given to break into the cafeteria. We would climb through the conveyor belt used for the dirty dishes during time of operation to get back where the goodies were. We would take our choice of Klondikes, ice cream sandwiches, popsicles and push-ups for extra snacks and treats.

Though it was frustrating and prevented us from further thefts, I made history there. I say this because even though we never got caught, one night we went down to commit our usual crime of ice cream theft, and a metal plate had been placed over the crack in the door that prevented us from using the ID card to open it. That night was scary because I thought we had been set up and expected to see staff arrive, when we realized that things had changed. When we saw the preventative measures they took, we immediately returned to the unit and escaped detection or so we thought. It just occurred to me that Rich was probably the one that put the metal plate over the door to prevent me from having any after-hours ice cream <grin>.

A big advantage to living at The Home for Crippled Children was that my family was a half a mile away, and I was about a mile from my high school. I had the best of both worlds because I was getting the structure and help I needed, and I could only spend a few minutes at home before having to return to the institution. I wasn't there long enough for craziness to happen, and I could retreat to the facility if/ when conflict began.

At the time, my father was a detective with the Pittsburgh Police and would talk to administrative staff about taking me out. This is the only place of the many different institutions I lived for seven of eight years of my childhood (9 years old – 17 years old) where my dad picked me up and took me out. And though it was limited, I was able to spend a little time with my childhood friends while attending my local high school with them and my two older brothers.

The greatest benefit of being at The Home for Crippled Children was being exposed to a group of kids that were as, or more disabled, than I. Like me, they had potential, were sensitive and wanted people to understand and care about them.

They, too, felt like rejects from their families and society. It would be unfair to say that all the patients there were not cared about, because many were; but many were not. I know, because we talked about these things. Not always in a mature way or in the right way. It was reflected in their anger and resistant behaviors following a phone call or because they saw others with visitors and they never got any.

Seeing the challenges that these kids were up against and fighting to get through every day gave me a sense of hope. Unfortunately, that never lasted very long because I frequently was feeling sorry for myself. I am very proud to have known these kids. I'm sure that many of them have done impressive and productive things with their lives since we were together. Regretfully, I never had contact with any of them since my stay there more than forty years ago.

The resilience, tenacity, strength and courage they showed every day was palpable. The qualities of these kids are what I remember more than I do their disabilities. I lived at the Home for Crippled Children, now The Children's Institute of Pittsburgh. I can say that I was proud to have done so. I say this because the disabled population is very supportive of one another. They know that the disability is only a fraction of the challenge. The social repercussions and societal alienation are far worse. We know that we need each other to weather the storm.

Warrendale Youth Development Center (YDC), and New Castle Youth Development Center (YDC) were run by the state of Pennsylvania. They were in Warrendale, PA and New Castle, PA, hence, Warrendale and New Castle YDC. Warrendale was like being a freshman or sophomore while New Castle was like being a junior or senior.

Warrendale Youth Development Center was where I stayed when I was fifteen years old. I was there for approximately ten months. This, too, had a bunch of buildings on a large piece of land that was between suburbia and outlying country land. If you wanted to abscond, you would have to travel a couple of miles just to get to the suburbs, turnpike or interstate #79 and hitchhike almost forty miles to get back to Pittsburgh. I did not run away from Warrendale YDC for these reasons. The local police were quite aware of the element (us) that was there and had an eye and ear out for "those delinquent kids at the youth development center."

I always wondered if it was because I was a big kid and my father was a cop, but other kids felt a need to fight me. I grew up fighting and was taught to fight at a young age, so that was not a problem for me. One of my brothers was a golden glove boxer. He and my father beat the heck out of me worse than these kids could. What I wasn't okay with was that I was being jumped by three and sometimes four kids at a time.

I wasn't okay with the punishment or the lack thereof that would follow and was pissed with staff members. I wondered if they were afraid of some of the kids there. Because of this, I, like them, became less caring about consequences, rules and how someone else felt. I became more and more bitter and depressed.

A few months after I had transitioned to this new place, I got a pleasant surprise. I looked and what I had imagined was about to happen. Yes, Mr. McIntosh and I would cross paths. I saw him on the grounds and knew that he was now a staff member at Warrendale YDC. He was a middle-aged guy when I was nine and at McIntyre Shelter, and I was now seeing him again six years later.

Both of us were six years older. By fifteen years of age, I was also six years angrier, was tipping the scale at about 200 pounds and was a very good athlete. I now had six more years of experience as a fighter. I had been abusing alcohol for about three years by then. I had been in several other institutions, and he must have found a new job at this institution where we finally crossed paths.

Another significant difference was that I no longer feared this man. In fact, I had thought about him many times over that six-year period and became livid every time. He did not work in the building I was staying in, but there was an administration building that everyone would have to enter for admission, to get their medications and many other things. I knew at some point, he and I would be face-to-face and I couldn't wait.

I'm not sure if he even recognized me. When I looked at him, hate and anger would circulate through me just as my blood did. I knew at some point we would be in the administration building at the same time. I was just hoping that it was sooner rather than later. I wanted to expose his cowardly heart whether it be from physically beating him down or exposing his fear of me in front of all the people that would be there. I knew I could hurt him if I had to, and that would be okay too.

The moment of truth came one day when I saw him walking with several kids toward the administration building. I knew that this was where I was going. I hoped that he would go up the stairs to the left. My heart began to beat a little faster as I saw him limp up the stairs. I was a couple hundred feet behind. I told some of the kids what he had done to me, and that they would want to watch closely. This was something they would not want to miss.

I entered the building with the other kids and the staff member who was supposed to be monitoring us. Mr. McIntosh and I made eye contact and were about ten feet apart. It was a crowded area, and I knew it was time. I looked at the kids I had prompted on the way into the building. My heart began to race, and my rage grew.

I said, "Hey, you coward bastard, do you remember me?" He pointed to his chest and looked at me wide-eyed and said, "Are you talking to me?" I looked around the room and everyone was wide-eyed. They couldn't believe that I was talking to this big man who was a staff member like this. That excited me even more. I reminded him that I was Jeff Parker, the kid who had a seizure when he worked at McIntyre Shelter. Instead of believing me and protecting me, he had assaulted me.

I told him that I was big enough and bad enough to defend myself today and had been looking forward to this moment for years. He said, "I can't fight you, I'm a staff member, and you know that." I said, "But you can bang a nine year old child's head off a desk three times?" I then told him, "I should take that damn wooden leg off and beat you with it, and then shove it up your ass."

By then several staff had come running to stand between us. They attempted to de-escalate the situation. The rage coursed through my veins. I then said, "Of all people, someone like you who has a disability should understand. You are a heartless piece of shit and should not be working with kids!"

This 250-pound man looked small and meek. I was so angry that I teared up but felt strong and accomplished as I had done what I had set out to do. That was to remove the façade he had built around his size and his authority as a staff member. Behind that was an insecure, angry and maybe even frightened person due to his disability. I knew that because I was the same way, but I would not abuse a child.

At that time, I would have preferred to physically assault him. The smiles, whispering and giggling that I saw from my peers' faces was what I imagined and even better when it did happen. I was sure that he had frightened some other kids there, whether it was because he was so big or because he, too, was different. After all, I knew firsthand that being different and particularly having a disability scares people.

Strangely enough, I do not remember what happened to Mr. McIntosh after that, and frankly I don't care. I was there for almost a year after this incident occurred and can't recall ever seeing him again. So, was he forced to resign or was he fired shortly after my tirade? Was he asked to leave once his coworkers and administrative staff found out that he abused a nine year old child? I don't remember the consequences for my actions that day, but I thought it was worth it.

Think about it, an incorrigible child just threatened to assault a staff member. I can assure you that they did not take that lightly. For some reason, I don't remember much after that. It's probably because I didn't care what the consequences would be. I exposed him in front of my peers and his coworkers. Though I don't believe in "closure", that was the closest I have been to finding it.

Though I was bitter then, I am not now. Just as I have outgrown certain pants and shirts, I have outgrown the anger, hate and resentment I once had for Mr. McIntosh. I wish him no harm, and it's all over and done with. Confronting him was a cathartic experience, and one I will never forget.

The experience was internally but not externally liberating because I was not free. I was still being confined. After nearly a year at Warrendale YDC, I graduated when I was transferred to New Castle YDC.

100

New Castle Youth Development Center was another facility that was run by the state of Pennsylvania or the County of Allegheny, (the government), just as Warrendale YDC and McIntyre Shelter were. All three of them were similar in that they all had a main building and many different cottage-like buildings where we lived. There was a cafeteria where we all went to eat, an administration building and an area for school classes. New Castle was a little different, however. As mentioned earlier, New Castle was the junior and senior years of the juvenile justice system so to speak.

The kids were older, bigger, stronger and a couple of years more callous and mean, as well as violent. Many had a couple of more years of crime on the streets of Pittsburgh. Numerous kids had graduated there from cutting classes and fighting, to stealing cars, carrying knives and guns. Some were there for allegedly committing murder, rape, attempted murder and aggravated assault.

For this reason, New Castle not only had the cottages but a large building with a fenced-in yard with an electric fence. Above the regular fence, was circular barbed wire at the top to prevent escape. This was for the kids that Judges Tambelli, Nelson and Jackson had put there for their offenses. It was called "Maximum Security" or as we called it "Max." Kids used to say, "Yeah, I just heard my boy was sent to "max." You never had to be at New Castle to know about "max." If you had been in institutions long enough, you knew what that meant.

Like the other places run by the government, there were a lot of sports and that was where I held my own. I was one of the best everywhere I went. In this regard, I was at least respected, if not liked by the other kids. I could hold my own in a fight as well, so that is why, like many other places, I was jumped when awake and attacked while asleep.

The "blanket party" was a low act that was physically and emotionally hurtful, but something happened at New Castle YDC that was far more offensive and violating. While sleeping, I had this warm stuff poured on my head. I woke up immediately and smelled something terrible. I then realized that it was at least a pint of urine. I later found that one or more kids donated a specimen that would be poured on my head while I was asleep. I never found out who did it. I also knew that no one would say because there was one huge kid there who basically ran the place.

I will refer to this person as "H" for huge. He was 17 years old like the rest of us, but he had to be about 6 feet, 4 inches tall and weighed well over 300 pounds. Everyone was afraid of him. I was a big and tough kid, and I feared him like no other. Not only was he huge, he was heartless and enjoyed terrorizing and hurting others. I don't believe I have ever feared anyone like I did "H". This guy terrorized me and many others. He had people working for him. He would order two or three of his cronies to do things to other kids in the cottages.

Following these incidents, I was in several fights in a short period of time. I figured if I fought at the drop of a hat, I would eventually beat the hell out of the person or persons that did this to me. Because of the fighting, and because I was terrified of big "H", I was transferred to a different cottage. I hid behind the fighting as the reason I was transferred, but was damn glad I didn't have to deal with big "H" anymore. I sure as hell wasn't going to fight him, so I am glad I got transferred.

The school we went to inside the institution was like all the others. They tried to stick to a curriculum, but we were being discharged from one place and being sent to another. Plus, we all were at various levels in our education as well as abilities. Many of us had learning disabilities. Some were mentally retarded. The term today might be "slow" or mentally "challenged." I can't keep up.

The school was called Frew Mill School. When one passed the GED test they could graduate. This would be the first time I can remember my father coming to see me when I was institutionalized. The previous visit to McIntyre Shelter was related to the abuse from Mr. McIntosh. That wasn't to visit me, but to beat the hell out of McIntosh or arrest him if action was not taken by the administration.

I barely passed my GED by 10-25 points. But as they say, 10 or 110, passing is passing. I was getting my diploma like anyone else, and I was darn proud. I remember it like it was yesterday because the keynote speaker was Judge Johnson. I don't remember much about his speech, but I remember the military uniform he wore. The whole left side of his chest was packed with various medals. There had to be at least thirty of them. His black shoes shined, so that you could use them to comb your hair. He was one impressive guy, and I am still glad I was never in front of him.

The guest speaker was Ted Needle, when he played for the Pittsburgh Steelers. He was as impressive 40 years ago as he is today. He is in the Football Hall of Fame for his achievements in the NFL. I saw him from that day forward as a Hall of Fame guy for the wonderful man that he is. I cannot remember specifically what he said, but I do remember that he was very encouraging. His message was a positive one. He was a young form of my mentor and dear friend, E. H. Like E., Ted Needle glowed and lit up a room when he entered it. He did not have a mean bone in his body and that was refreshing.

All of us received our diploma while wearing the cap and gown. The whole official thing took place, and it was great. A very uncommon thing happened that day. Outside of my success with sports, I don't remember feeling proud of myself, but that day I was. Unfortunately, being proud of myself was not something that was going to happen again for many years, outside of sports.

I spent about a year of my life in New Castle YDC. It seemed like a lot longer because it was a nightmare. I have no idea what ever happened to that huge kid, "H", but I would not be surprised to hear that he is dead or in prison. However, I believe in miracles and that God can do anything.

I mentioned earlier how proud I was when I graduated with a GED. I had this weird kind of pride over being able to drink like a fish. That is why I spent a lot of time in "the drunk tank" as an adult.

The Drunk Tank--Throughout most of my 20s, I paid many visits to the drunk tank. There were two drunk tanks in the City of Pittsburgh during my drinking days. One was in the downtown area, and the other was in the North Side neighborhood. There were jail cells inside of the two precincts for drunks like me, who had been arrested for minor things like public intoxication or drunk and disorderly. Early on, most of my visits were to the downtown precinct.

When the police had a busy evening with drunks, and the downtown station became filled, they would take the rest of us across the Allegheny River to the North Side station. I spent many nights sleeping off the booze, but that's just an expression because I didn't sleep much. There was an iron or steel bed, a commode and a sink, and that was it.

The cell often smelled like any of the different liquids and fluids that can come from our body and were often unflushed. Sometimes, it was even worse because a previous visitor had used the sink. I was there all seasons of the year, but it was far more unpleasant during the summer months when the temperature and humidity were up.

The officers that worked the drunk tanks knew that my father was a Lieutenant of the Pittsburgh Police, and many knew me by name. The actor, Hal Smith, played Otis Campbell, who was the town's drunk in the little town of Mayberry on the Andy Griffith Show. He was well known in town by the civilians and the police, played by Don Knotts and Andy Griffith.

I remember an episode where Otis walked into the police station drunk, went into the open cell and locked himself in while giving and receiving friendly greetings. That is a bit of a stretch but not as much as you might think. Unlike Otis, there was not the friendly greetings part, but like Otis, there was the familiarity with public drunkenness and frequent visits to the drunk tank.

As mentioned at the opening of this book, my intentions are not to tell "war stories" about my life experiences, but it is important that information is included to give perspective as to how things were back then. I would be remiss to not mention a column written about me in The Pittsburgh Press. It went something like this, *Jeffrey Parker, son of Pittsburgh Police Lieutenant, William Parker, has been incarcerated for public intoxication 29 times in the last nine months.*

I was drinking heavily, acting like a fool and getting in trouble back in those days. It's not something I am proud of. At that time, I did not care about much of anything other than playing sports and drinking as much as I could. My father read *The Pittsburgh Press* daily. He was not happy when he read this. In fact, he was infuriated. Having a "good name" in the community was important to him.

He had served in WWII, worked in the local steel mills and had served the public for more than 30 years by the time he retired from the police force. He did not want his drunken son to taint his reputation. He was even more upset when I began to get arrested and be incarcerated in the Allegheny County Jail.

Allegheny County Jail--I was arrested and incarcerated in the Allegheny County Jail three times, maybe four if my memory is correct. The longest stay there was 30 days. I was in a certain part of the jail referred to as "The Shoe." I was in a holding cell until I was bailed out after a day or two. I was in the hospital section of the jail twice because of my severe seizure disorder. I was in withdrawal from alcohol both times and having severe seizures because of it. For this reason, hospital care was required so that I could be attended to twenty-four hours a day.

The seizures alone were a nightmare. To be having them while being locked up in a not so friendly environment was very unpleasant and made me feel vulnerable. I'm sure I had minor bumps and bruises from the simple assault charges I had, but you should have seen the other guy. Other times, I had to be attended to because of a fight with the cement, as my father called it. Those I lost.

I have several summary and misdemeanor offenses but have never been convicted of a felony. My convictions were primarily for simple assaults and possession of a small amount of marijuana. After all, I never had enough money to buy or possess large quantities of weed. The convictions resulted in one- and two-year probation sentences and were all within a four-year period. In addition to the probation, other stipulations would include addiction and mental health therapy. This is also referred to as Dual Diagnosis treatment.

I certainly did not want to be locked up, but probation was a pain in the butt. The therapy was no big deal because I had been in therapy most of my life. I still see a trauma therapist today, but this is by choice. It's different when one is forced by the courts to get help. That is what I needed though and I believe then and now, that people who are forced to go to treatment can still benefit.

My two most serious charges were robbery and aggravated assault. Though it was robbery by the definition of the law, the charge was laughed at by the judge and then thrown out of court. The aggravated assault was different. It was far more serious. I went to trial and could be facing four to seven years of imprisonment. Thank goodness the judge looked at the evidence and not at my history before deciding that I was not guilty for reason of self-defense.

The robbery charge came on a bright summer afternoon. There are several bakery shops on the street I hung out at. I saw someone who owed me money for quite a while. It was only ten or twenty dollars but that is a lot of money when you're on a fixed income and need a drink to take the edge off the hangover from the night before.

As he exited the bakery, I asked him for the money he had owed me for several weeks. When he said no, the cake he was carrying was snatched from his hands. He pled with me to give his cake back. I told him that if he gave me my money, he could have his cake back. Right when I snatched his cake, the police were traveling down the street and witnessed the whole thing. I was arrested and charged with robbery.

While sitting in the county jail, word got around about what I did to get the robbery charge. It became known as "the Cake Caper." Today I can't help but laugh at that one. The only one I can think of that is even close to that crime happened in downtown Pittsburgh, following the World Series victory in 1979. I have a friend that attended that championship game and like me he was young and dumb. To celebrate, he began pulling bushes out of the ground and was arrested for some stupid charge like disorderly conduct, vandalism or something like that. My friend (whom I choose to keep anonymous) was nicknamed "The Landscaper."

As many childhood friends do, he moved out of the area, and we went many years without contact. As many childhood friends also do, we reconnected via social media. We eventually, talked on the phone to catch up after many years. While reminiscing, I referred to him as *The Landscaper*, and he referred to me as *The Cake Caper*. I laughed almost uncontrollably because neither of us missed a beat. After all those years, we remembered our mutually embarrassing moment with great laughter.

On the more serious side of things, the aggravated assault charge was scary. One sunny afternoon, I was sitting in the backyard of my apartment and drinking. A friend of mine showed up with his friend with liquor, and we all began to drink. We drank the liquor and chased it with beer. Before long, it was all gone, and an argument started. I was disgusted, and after a few choice words were exchanged, I turned to walk back into my apartment building when I was hit from behind. I did the best I could to defend myself. It was then that I was kicked right under my chin. The force of the kick lifted all 250 pounds of me into the air, and I landed a couple of feet from where I had been.

Survival mode kicked in and before I knew it, I was running around the outside of the fence toward the front of my apartment building. I thought, "Wow! This is a miracle. Am I really running?" You see, less than a year earlier, I had a cervical fusion operation, and here I had just been kicked in my chin and lifted off the ground. Apparently, my neurosurgeon was as good as I had heard.

Both were chasing me. As I got around the corner of the fence, I looked behind me, and there was only one of them. This was because the other had jumped over the fence and into the yard. When I came around to the front walk, the one who had jumped over the fence was standing in front of me, and the other was gaining ground behind me.

What neither of them knew was that while they were pounding me and kicking me, I had retrieved a small pocket knife out of my pant leg. While being confronted by the one in front of me, and before he realized that I was holding a knife, I told him to get out of my way. Right then, he lunged at me. I swung the knife and accidentally cut his neck, though I did not know it at the time. As I ran up the front stairs to get into the building, I looked behind me and the guy who had been chasing behind me was holding the one that I had cut.

I immediately called 911 to have them arrested for assaulting me. The police, however, weren't hearing it, and I was the one arrested. While in handcuffs, I was taken to the hospital. I found out that he was taken to the same hospital. I was told that he had lost a lot of blood and might not make it. I had so many different thoughts and feelings going on.

They may have initiated the fight, and I too was badly hurt, but I still felt bad about what happened. I was terrified at the thought of him dying. I had known this person since he was a little child, and I was very close to his aunt and uncle. And of course, there was the thought of being in jail for a very long time, even though I was defending myself.

People have often asked what the turning point in my life was, and two things immediately come to mind. The first was the death of my father. I had to grow up quickly, and begin to take care of myself and stay out of trouble as he wasn't around to save me anymore. When I needed someone to bail me out or needed money for whatever reason, including an attorney like this time, he was around to pay for one. This time he would not be. The second reason is that I could have gone to jail for a long time and as usual, the problem stemmed from being drunk.

What makes these two things even more pertinent and life-changing is that they both happened within a short period of one another. In fact, the initial trial had to be postponed so that I could attend my father's funeral. I remember the funeral provided for my father where many of the Pittsburgh Police were in attendance. I remember the gunshots going off and the flag being folded up and handed to my paternal grandmother.

My father may not have been the greatest dad due to the physical and verbal abuse sometimes. However, he was an honorable man who had served his country in WWII and his community as a Lieutenant of the Pittsburgh Police Force. He served his family by taking us in after he and my mother's divorce. He had rescued us from the projects and given us a home in one of the nicer neighborhoods in the city.

My brother, who is an excellent musician, played *Taps* with his saxophone to honor my father. There wasn't a dry eye in the cemetery, including the police officers who were there to honor him. A friend of mine, who never shows an emotion other than laughter and anger, had tears running down his face. This was a very sad but also a very proud moment for me, and a moment I will never forget. My father was one hell of a man and lived a very complete life.

On the other hand, here I am awaiting trial on aggravated assault charges and being a drunk. My honorable father was being put in the ground when I was thirty years old. I had been drinking for almost twenty years. I had been on welfare or SSI all my adult life. I only had two or three jobs to that point and none of them had lasted. I knew that something had to change. But first, I had to see how my future was going to be decided by a judge, in just a short time after burying my father.

The terrifying day came. I had decided on a judge instead of a jury trial. Not sure why but that's what I did. Maybe the fairness I had from

108

Judge Tambelli, when I was a juvenile, had something to do with that and maybe not. It was now time for both sides to present their case. The judge would decide if I was guilty or not guilty despite the fact that he was not there and didn't see what had happened. I didn't know who or what he would believe.

I couldn't help but think about what we did when in Juvenile Court. We would say, "What if he didn't get laid last night or had an argument with his wife this morning and is in a bad mood?" That thought scared me. All I could think was, let's get this over with. The anticipatory anxiety was driving me crazy on the one hand, but on the other, I didn't want to start because I am still free now and may not be later.

The alleged victim had the advantage because I was the one arrested. He had his friend, who helped him to assault me, there to testify on his behalf. I was the one with the knife. My wounds had healed, and many were covered with my hair. Although his wound had healed too, the scar on his neck was long and visible from a distance. It looked as serious as they had said, the night it happened.

Thank goodness that my mother is as smart as she is because, without the pictures she had taken of my head and the trail of blood drops from the back of the building to the front, I wouldn't have had a chance. Because of this and the medical records she had brought showing the care I required that evening, the judge was able to see the seriousness of my wounds. I was a very negative person, however, and could not imagine something going in my favor. I believed this was going to be the time I went to prison as I had been told many times over the years.

When the time came for the verdict, I was terrified. The judge had to further the anticipation by telling the three of us involved that this is what happens when a group of people get together and get drunk. He went on to say something like, "You were friends and now you're not. Before the incident, there were no injuries and after, both were injured significantly." I'm thinking to myself, "Please give me the answer!"

He went on to say something like, "I find the defendant, Jeffrey Parker NOT GUILTY for the reason of SELF-DEFENSE." He explained the reason for his decision. This is all paraphrasing from almost thirty years ago, but the determining factor was that the alleged victim's wound was a slash and not a gouge. He further explained that, this showed that it was a defense move made by the defendant. If he were the aggressor, it would have been a gouge if he had stuck the knife in him.

When he had completed his explanation, I was so relieved and so emotionally drained. This meant that I got to return to my college studies at our local Community College of Allegheny County (CCAC). I hoped to complete what I had started to honor my father and start a different life. I had enrolled at CCAC earlier in the year. I took a chance, that if not convicted, I would be able to return to school rather than go to prison. Being acquitted was extremely motivating. I will always remember that had it gone the other way, my life would have been entirely different.

It was an awakening experience. I frequently look at things today based on the predicament I was in. I ask myself if I want my destiny to be determined by me or by someone else? I don't want my freedom being based on whether someone is in a good or bad mood. This has worked wonders for me over the years and has helped me to stay busy and out of trouble. I have worked hard to think before I act. I continue setting goals, doing the right thing, and not becoming complacent. If I stick to this solid foundation, it's not only possible but probable that I will stay out of trouble and be a productive citizen. This is not at all possible if I return to drugs or alcohol.

SECTION III

Relationships

Family

Relationships play a significant role in our lives whether they are good or bad, healthy or unhealthy. In my earlier years, I was drawn toward those like me, the alienated, outcasts and badly behaved. These were the kids with whom I was most comfortable. Most couldn't understand why a kid would want to do just the opposite of what their parents told them to do even when they were getting ready to do it before being told.

We were rebellious, that's why. We were incorrigible, that's why. Today the term incorrigible is politically incorrect, and I'm not sure what they call it today. The person, that used to be referred to as a janitor, is now called a sanitation engineer, so who knows what incorrigible has turned into. But kids don't become this way with no real explanation.

There are exceptions, but in general, children are loveable and want to please their parents. When this is not the case there is usually a reason. Many of us were physically, verbally, emotionally and sexually abused. The child might be neglected of basic needs including love and affection. Kids are often a product of their environment because they regurgitate and imitate what they hear and see.

Sexual abuse is not openly discussed if it did happen, but I know it happens because of my own personal experiences. As a psychotherapist,

I have heard horror stories that clearly explain why people have mental health and addiction problems. I began physically running away when I was just seven years old. By the time I was twelve, I was running away by using and abusing alcohol and marijuana. Even today, this is not an easy thing to discuss, but particularly for boys and men.

Many of us had a learning disability and frequently cut classes. When we didn't get the support, love and positive reinforcement we needed, the self-esteem we already had decreased, and there were many that were bullied far more than I. These factors weeded us out (and we were the weeds). Through this process a subculture of kids was developed.

We began getting high, drinking and fighting at a young age. Many of us were reluctant to go home. We didn't feel loved or like we belonged anywhere except with one another. This only reinforced what everyone already thought and many of us heard from our own family members. I could not count the number of times that I was referred to as a loser or was told that, "You are going to be a drunk and never do anything with your life. Countless times I was told, "You will be in and out of jail all of your life." The one that hurt the most was being told by my father, "I disown you. You are no longer my son." I eventually became desensitized to it. I did the best I could to block the hurt out. I stopped caring when I heard it and numbed it with alcohol and marijuana.

In one sense, being part of the incorrigible subculture gave me an identity. It felt like this was where I belonged. My self-destructive behaviors were taking me down a dark path that would make it nearly impossible to ever be anything but a drunk, an epileptic, a loser, an outcast and an under-achiever. Positive relationships were not there and when they aren't, you go where you are accepted. For me, that was the street.

I remember when a negative, unhealthy relationship was far better to me than no relationship at all. I hated being alone, and that's the bottom line. Someone explained to me years ago that the reason I hate being alone is because I don't like the company I am with. This was one of the most powerful things I had ever heard, and it was true. Today, I enjoy being alone, and it is not to escape like those that isolate. I spend time alone to relax and regroup with the full intention of going back out into the world and contributing. On the other hand, those that isolate are trying to avoid their world and the challenges in it.

An inordinate number of people who I grew up with were part of this subculture that became fatalities due to drugs and alcohol. They became numbers and statistics for the murders, suicides and accidental deaths from overdosing and car accidents. Nearly 70 people I grew up with and who used drugs and alcohol have passed away. For some reason, I am still alive and today, I am very particular with whom I spend time.

I would rather be alone than be with someone who is not good for me. During my long and dark journey called life, there have always been special relationships that I cherished and were positive. They were relationships with people who were "normal" and did not spin out-of-control. Unlike us, they responded to their adversities in ways that made them stronger, more functional and successful in life.

In this chapter, I will give a little background information about my relationships with each special friend, followed by their input about their first impressions of me, my recovery process and our present relationship.

<u>Family</u> – You can't choose who your family members are going to be. However, you do have a choice how you will treat one another, and how much you will and will not associate with them, particularly as adults.

How can I talk about relationships without talking about my family relationships and the family system? Out of respect for my siblings, what I will share will be a little vague but will be enough for you to get the picture.

I'd like to begin by saying that there was a lot of love in my family. However, there was as much or more dysfunction and even hate. This may not be politically correct by today's standards, but it's my family and my story so I will stick with dysfunctional.

How dysfunctional? I remember trying family therapy when I was about 9 or 10 years old. I tell people who ask if I was ever in family therapy (including my clients/patients) that it was a very short-term experience. We were able to complete one session without the paramedics or police being called.

We went back for a second session. The therapist saw us coming down the hall, and I could see her say, "Oh my God, it's the Parkers." She went to the second story window of her office, opened it and jumped. Not quite, but that isn't far from the truth.

My parents were married about ten years when they were divorced. I was just three or four years old when the divorce was finalized. My middle brother was four or five and our eldest brother was eight or nine years old. My eldest brother was separated from us when he went to live with our grandparents in Kentucky. The two youngest stayed with our mother and lived in the Rankin Projects. I heard over the years, that dad took it hard and licked his wounds while living alone in a duplex apartment.

My father "took us in," in the summer of 1968 when he bought a house in one of the nicer areas in the city of Pittsburgh, Pennsylvania. Dad had been living in a duplex (in this same area) since he and mom got divorced. I was told by both parents that dad took it hard and lost weight because of it. I guess he pulled out of it because he decided to buy a house and have his three kids move in with him.

Dad was looking like the hero at that time but at other times not so much. I remember standing outside of Building C at the Hawkins Village Projects waiting for him to pick us up for the weekend, and he never showed.

When we lived in the projects, mom was working two and sometimes three jobs and still had trouble paying bills. Dad accused her of being poor because she did not use her money wisely. She told us when we got older that the financial problems were because he wasn't paying much in child support, and it wasn't uncommon for him to miss or skip a payment. As they say, there's one side, the other, and then there is the truth. I didn't care because the one truth was that they were divorced, and no one was happy about it.

Mom would say that dad did not give enough for us to live on in the first place. She said that it wasn't worth fighting it because he was a police officer and knew the right people. That was why she never took him to court. She also said that the divorce was ugly enough, and she didn't want to go through it.

We were in the projects for about two or three years when my mother became ill. Her medical and financial problems made it impossible for her to take care of us. My father decided to buy a house and took all three of us in. Dad asked his mother (our Grammy) to move in and help take care of the house and the three of us while he worked full time as a Lieutenant of the Pittsburgh Police Force.

It was easy to forget him missing payments and not showing up when your hero tells you that you can all live with him in a new house in a beautiful neighborhood. The new neighborhood looked even more attractive after living in the projects. Our new home was the opposite of oppressed, congested, poor and unsafe.

I remember flying over the new house like it was yesterday. My dad had a friend who had his own airplane, and he flew us over the new house. It was one of those unforgettable moments, particularly for a kid six years old. I remember looking down and seeing this tiny row of houses (that was our entire block). I was still able to distinguish the next to the last one before this humongous school that would be two doors down from where I was now going to live. Dad, you're the best!!

Neither my mother nor my father ever remarried. With dad being a cop, and every month alternating through all three shifts, it made it difficult for him to raise us alone. He asked his mother, our "Grammy" to move in and help with the housework and with raising her three grandchildren.

Claudette Parker

My Mom

Most of the information about my relationship with my mother was brought to light in the earlier chapters when I was having a really hard time in my day-to-day life with seizures, depression and alcoholism. Like many children, my mother was my primary protector who showed unconditional love daily.

In addition to the loving and protecting, she was wise, self-confident and assertive. My mother knew firsthand about trauma, betrayal and abuse. She was born in Kentucky with her fraternal twin brother, Claude. I always loved their names, Claude and Claudette.

Both of their biological parents were alcoholics, and their mother died when they were very young. My mother and Uncle Claude had two other siblings, an older brother and a younger sister. When their biological father was deemed unfit to take care of them, the oldest sibling was adopted by their biological grandparents. My mom and Uncle Claude were adopted by one family and their little baby sister, another.

Their eldest brother, Uncle Phil, died from alcoholism while in his mid-thirties. My mother explained that other than Uncle Phil, the three of them were placed in an orphanage when she and her twin were six years old, and their baby sister was a year old. My mother described that painstaking day when her little baby sister was taken from her arms in the orphanage and adopted by a family in Ohio. My mother would have an endless search for more than thirty-five years, before she found her "baby sister."

I remember how happy she was after waiting all those years, quickly followed by disappointment. It seemed that my mother was far happier and more willing to stay in touch with her little sister than her little sister was. Her sister had moved out years earlier and lived in California. She returned to Ohio occasionally to see her parents. Mom hoped to renew the relationship for life with her little sister, but it never turned out that way. She still benefited from finding her because it gave her a feeling of completeness.

My mother and my Uncle Claude were fortunate enough to be adopted by an older couple, who we referred to as "Nunna and Puppup." My Puppup was offered a position at the *Pittsburgh Press* as Director of Circulation, and mom and Uncle Claude relocated to the City of Pittsburgh. Shortly thereafter, they adopted an infant girl who is my Aunt Barbara.

When they got older, Uncle Claude and Aunt Barbara moved down to Kentucky, which is also where Nunna and Puppup retired to. They had a beautiful home and about 14 acres of land in Junction City, Kentucky. All of mom's family had gathered together in Kentucky and lived there for many years. We stayed in Pittsburgh. I remember how painful this was for her. I also remember how devastated she was when her biological brother died from alcoholism.

When I look back now, I can only imagine how painful it was to see her son on the verge of drinking himself to death at an early age, and that is no exaggeration. When I was young, it was the many crises that brought my mother and I close. She was so protective of me and knew how vulnerable I was due to my seizures, depression and alcoholism.

In the earlier years, when we lived in the projects, mom did anything and everything to make the best of it. I remember her using a washboard to scrub our clothes so that we would have clean clothes to go to school. Her hands and knuckles would become cracked and dry. I remember her knuckles bleeding when she accidentally nicked them on the washboard.

I would put her in the Martha Stewart category because she would do anything and everything. She could make home-cooked meals to warm our stomachs and our hearts. If she needed to get fancy, she could make gourmet dishes. In fact, for a while she catered parties for as many as 300 people. She did all the shopping, preparation, cooking, decoration of the tables and more.

Mom could fix her car or change the tire if she had a flat. When she moved (which was frequently), she carried furniture up flights of stairs. I remember watching her lay shag carpet throughout the first floor of this big country home in Gibsonia, Pennsylvania that she decided to rent. The home looked like a barn on the outside and not much better on the inside. She spackled the walls and ceiling and then painted everything. The outside still looked like a barn but when mom was done with the interior, you thought you were in the home of a millionaire.

She could crochet an afghan for a king size bed in three days. She would make several of them and then go down the parkway, pull off on the shoulder, get out of the car and climb up and under a bridge to give the afghans to the homeless people that were living there during the cold Pittsburgh winter months.

She took part in the efforts to have Prisoners of War (POWs) returned home by having hundreds if not thousands of people sign petitions to get them home. Those Missing in Action (MIAs) made her heart ache as well.

My mother had a heart of gold and tried to help anyone and everyone she could, especially me. She not only helped me with everyday things, but she saved my life. We were on the phone one afternoon, and I was sick and tired of everything. I made a remark that I just couldn't take it anymore or something like that. She did not give it much thought at the time or she would have interrogated me about it. Apparently, she did not forget what I said because hours later, I drank an entire bottle of my newly refilled prescription of Dilantin, 100 mgs pills.

Dilantin is an anti-seizure anticonvulsant medication. I was being prescribed six - 100 mg capsules a day and therefore, was getting 180 a month. I took about six handfuls of thirty, with each handful being gulped with a mouth full of Nikolai Vodka. This was not my first time, nor would it be my last.

As time passed, my thoughts about leaving this earth could become a reality. I washed down all 180 of the Dilantin, 100 mg pills with a liter of vodka in about an hour. She had called a couple of hours after our earlier conversation and did not get an answer. So, she called again. Mom later told me that when I didn't answer the second time, she knew something was wrong. She got in her car and drove to my apartment as quickly as possible. She arrived to find me on my bed unconscious. She said my breathing was very shallow, and my heart rate was extremely low.

She immediately called #911 and to spare me the humiliation, she cleaned my apartment as best she could before the EMTs arrived. They put a sleeve of some kind on my leg and pumped it so that blood could be pumped up to my head and heart. I was rushed to the emergency room and was in the Intensive Care Unit (ICU) for several days before I was in the clear. The doctors told me that I was near death and without question my mother had saved my life.

I remember being so grateful in one way, but in another way upset with her for saving me. It meant I had to continue living in this miserable world with my miserable life. It became almost routine for mom to come over and check on me at my apartments over the years to see if I was okay.

She lived about ten minutes away and would drive over and sometimes, just stand outside of my apartment door until she heard me snoring, before she would go home and sleep. The times when she came over, and I was not at my apartment, she would go back home and just pray and cry and hope for the best until she could no longer keep her eyes open.

My mother had already lost five children. She had four miscarriages and one stillborn. Mom said that that was why she was so devastated when my father bought the house and took us in after their divorce. She said that, "All I ever wanted to do was be a mom and have a big family. I wanted to make meals and take care of my husband and children." When I was in the throes of my addiction, I did not understand the depths of turmoil, worry, stress and God knows what else, that I was putting her through.

A) She was taken from her biological parents because of alcoholism. Alcohol led to the deaths of her mother in her late twenties and her brother in his mid-late thirties.

B) A very difficult and adversarial divorce

C) The loss of five children at birth

D) She had her biological sister (who was an infant at the time), taken from her arms in the orphanage when she was just six years old.

E) All of mom's family, including her twin brother and their little sister all moved to Kentucky. She was the lone family member left here in Pittsburgh, Pennsylvania.

With her background and family support being hundreds of miles away, her son is out in the street or in the bar trying to drink himself to death or he is taking a bottle of pills with it. He is getting into fights and going to the emergency room for very serious wounds and alcohol toxicity with an alcohol blood level of 0.5. How selfish and unthoughtful is that?

My poor mom had already had so many terrible and painful losses in her life. Here I was trying to become another. Her son, whom she had dedicated her life to protecting and trying to provide for is seemingly trying to cause her more pain day after day.

I was very manipulative like most substance abusers and would exploit her love, sympathy and concern for me without even realizing it most of the time. It's human nature to take someone as far as they will allow you. I played on the strings of her sympathy because she knew firsthand the hell I was going through, and how much I was struggling. She knew that I was searching for relief. So even when I did something wrong, she would make excuses for me and enable me.

She had to be hurting as much as I was and maybe more. There was nothing that she could do but watch me self-destruct and then go pick up the pieces and put them back together. What was my response? It was to propel myself further into the pit. Mom would come to my rescue time and time again.

When we are actively using drugs and/or alcohol, we do not think of the pain we are causing others. It might be in the back of our minds. There may be a lot of guilt and shame from the past, but I was not in tune enough to realize the full gist of what I was doing to her. I thought even less about how it was impacting other people that loved me. Every day, my mission was to escape and that was my focus. Everything else was on the periphery.

The following is an example of this. I remember it as if it happened yesterday. I was just under three years sober and had my Master's Degree and had been working for a little more than two years. I was now a professional, white collar worker. I had a nice apartment, and things were getting better every day. I told mom that I didn't want to catch her returning my Christmas gift and to just tell me what she wanted for Christmas. I would get it for her.

She looked at me with her precious warm smile. Her big bright brown eyes were twinkling with joy and she said, "Son, you already gave me the greatest present I could ask for." I asked her what she was talking about because I hadn't seen her in a while. I knew that I had yet to buy her a Christmas present. She said, "I don't have to come to the hospital or jail to visit you anymore. Now I can sleep at night. I don't have to worry about you or about the police showing up at my door to tell me that you were found dead somewhere. That is the greatest present you could ever give to me."

Unfortunately, the stronger and more independent I became, the further we grew apart. She always wanted the best for me. When I began to exceed anything I had ever imagined, mom kind of faded from my life, and that intimate relationship was lost.

She told me that while growing up with Uncle Claude and Aunt Barb, she did not get the attention they did because she did not misbehave. She said that they never did anything bad like me and my brothers did. They did typical kids' stuff that drew the attention of their parents to them and away from her. Ironically, that is exactly what she had done. When I was drinking and going to the hospital, institutions and jail when I got older, we were close, and she was always there. It was as if I no longer served a purpose for her because I wasn't doing anything wrong anymore and was not in crisis. She didn't have to save me anymore.

To put things in perspective, my wife and I bought a house, and I was on cloud nine. Three months later, we had our cozy little wedding of about 50-60 people as we took our vows from the local magistrate in front of the fireplace of our living room. My mother was in attendance of course. But, other than staying with us briefly, because she had to when she lost her housing, she never stepped foot in our home again during the last ten years of her life.

She was her wonderful self and paid for a celebration held for my graduation from Community College where I got an AS in Criminal Justice, and specifically, Corrections Administration. There were about 50 family and friends to celebrate my graduation. I was now the first one in my family to ever graduate from college (even though it was a 2-year degree).

As I progressed in my education, mom progressed in her illness to many medical problems and hoarding. She was not going out as much, and little by little, became more and more indigent and isolative. I seldom saw my mother in the last 15 years of her life. It was not by choice. I would make efforts to see her or go out with her, but she was not interested. She was struggling to get from one day to the next. She was not interested in going out to have dinner or a cup of coffee.

At the very beginning of our fading relationship, I was confused and could not understand why the woman to whom I owed everything for her immeasurable love and support was not interested in spending time with me. I had caused her such heartache over the years. I wanted her to see the new me and come over to my house so that I could cook for her.

I had degrees, was working and taking care of myself and was seizure-free and sober. It was like she didn't want anything to do with me. I learned over the years that you cannot force anyone to do anything. If she wanted to reject my offers time after time, there was nothing that I could do about it. It made me very sad. I had pictured us getting together and having normal adult conversations over a nice dinner once I had got my life together, but it was not to be.

My wife and I like to cook out on the grill, and we have a big backyard. We would invite her over to spend time with us and our dogs in the backyard and have some steaks or burgers. She never accepted the offer. It felt like I was being punished for getting a life and not getting into trouble anymore, but I learned to live with it as I had so many other things.

There was no dislike or hate between us. When we were together, we usually got along after I got my life together, but there wasn't much because we never spent time together. I was hurt but knew there was a reason. I could see that as she and I grew apart, she was magnetized toward my two brothers. She was far more involved with them than me. This was likely because they were still struggling. One had a serious addiction and mental health problems, as I had for so many years, and the other was often in crisis for his own reasons.

My mother was drawn to conflict, problems and crises (which my two siblings and she were still having), and I wasn't. It began to make perfect sense that her attention would be drawn toward them and not me. She now had to go rescue them because I was doing well. Like many other things in life, I learned to live with it. After all, I had tried to engage with her and spend time with her, but she seemed to be in a different world. Was I now in a different world? It was both.

The dynamic between my mother and I was like that of friends I used to party with. When I was getting high and drunk with them every day, they were my friends. When I stopped using, we seemed to have nothing in common, and they had no interest in spending time with me. The only difference was that the common "drug" for my mother and I had been problems and crises. When the problems and crises were gone, she didn't need me anymore. As sick as it sounds, when people are codependent, the rescuer depends on the "problem child" to provide crises and turmoil.

It's like a normal family where the empty nest syndrome inevitably comes. The children leave home. The parents have trouble adapting early on because the children were the main part of the parents' lives, and they are no longer there. It's quite common for the parents to begin questioning what their purpose in life is now that the children are gone.

Along those same lines, my mother's entire life was spent rescuing me. When I had finally rescued myself and learned to live a clean and sober lifestyle, she must have felt like she no longer had a purpose. She assured me that this was not the case, but the disintegration of our relationship said something else.

The bottom line is that when I really needed my mother, she was there. For that I will always be grateful. I remember having an argument with my mother when I told her that the biggest fear of my whole life was losing her. She had prepared me well for that moment because with the lack of time we spent together, it was as if she had already passed away. The pain from growing apart over the years was significant, but my words that day were prophetic.

I say this because as my mom's health deteriorated, as did the long-term care facilities where she would live, a role reversal occurred. In the terminology of addiction, my mom was the typical *enabler,* and our relationship was the typical example of *co-dependence.*

This is not to place blame on my mother but on me. This is because she could not have enabled me if I did not take advantage of her and of the opportunities she gave me to do so. I have patients that have told me that their parents not only gave them money but also drove them where they needed to go to get drugs.

In doing so, the parent (or whoever the enabler might be), truly believes that they are helping by preventing their child from going through withdrawal. As strange as it may seem to those who are fortunate and have not been in this situation, it makes perfect sense to those in the internal battles of addiction.

I could depend on mom to defend me, if someone were judgmental about me and my drunken behaviors. Despite her financial woes, when I chose alcohol over having food in my refrigerator, she would show up at my apartment with more food than I knew what to do with. How did I thank her? I answered the door hungover from the night before and ready to drink myself into oblivion later that night.

I was on disability due to all the things that were wrong with me like alcoholism, depression, PTSD and more. I was responsible enough to pay my rent first thing, but after that, it was difficult to decide what money should go toward buying cigarettes, booze or whatever else. The problem was that my rent was about 40% of my disability check.

The rent was a "no brainer" because my two biggest fears in life are being homeless and being locked up in jail. My dear mother made these decisions a lot easier though. When she supplied the food there was no choice because now that I had food, the rest of my money could be spent on liquor and cigarettes.

So even though she was not giving me money directly to buy liquor with, she was giving it to me indirectly. My mother was a very intelligent woman, so intellectually, she had to have known that. But addiction is referred to as a family disease. Just as the substance abusing person seems to live in a brain freeze with little logic, so too, do family members sometimes.

This reminds me of when I voluntarily asked my mother to be my payee. A payee is someone that holds the person's money for them to make sure that the money is going toward things that are needed and not drugs, alcohol and cigarettes. She, initially, said that she didn't want to because she knew that it would be nothing short of a nightmare. We talked and came to an agreement. I was sincere about adhering to the conditions of the agreement at the time. But as an addict who is being honest about it, that changes.

I would try to get her to bend a little, but she stood strong early on. Eventually, the more she resisted my request for more money the more heated the arguments became. She would ask me what the money was for. Of course, I would become defensive and tell her that it was my money and I could do what I wanted with it. She would remind me that I came to her and asked for her help and that she initially declined for this exact reason.

The time came when we agreed that this wasn't going to work. The reason it didn't work was because, although my intentions were good at the beginning, I wasn't ready to stop drinking or smoking, and she was just doing what I had asked her. The other two reasons were because she did not need or deserve all the extra commotion and conflict. I wanted access to my money so that I could drink and smoke when I wanted.

Mom was never financially sound but had a wealth of knowledge, thoughtfulness, love and support. She always put her own needs last and others' first. Mom never had much of a life because it always focused on her kids or on helping and doing for others. When she wasn't intervening because I was in crisis, she was trying to console me and convince me that things would get better. What I was going through would be used in a good way some day.

My mom was a religious woman and a student of the bible. It is where she found her peace, because it sure was not coming from the family. Mom used to tell me that, "God is going to use all of this in a special way to touch and inspire other people who are lonely, poor and suffering from disabilities just as you are."

I'm not terribly sure if I have inspired any, let alone many. What I do know is that today, I am in a position where I can make a difference. There are opportunities for public speaking engagements, writing this book, teaching, counseling and being a board member at my college instead of being an active substance user and abuser.

I am, in fact, clean and sober and working, for the last twenty years or so, with those that have substance use and mental health disorders. I am listening today to what she had told me years ago, and that is to use my experiences to help and benefit others. This is what I had in mind when I went to school and decided what field I wanted to work in. It is also why I chose this project.

I also know that her words helped to inspire me to tap into painful memories in hopes of reaching people and letting them know that there is hope and that anything is possible. Though things didn't turn out the way I would have liked them to, my mother was there for me when I really needed her.

Thank God, she lived long enough to see the results of her wisdom, guidance and support throughout the many years of turmoil. My mother passed away on my tenth wedding anniversary which was October 14, 2016. I will always believe that she stuck around long enough to see my wife and me match the ten years married that she and father had, only mine is still going and the quality of it much better than hers. I think she would agree.

I also believe that it was a miracle that she was able to tolerate, endure and survive one crisis after another and be there to rescue, support and unconditionally love her sons. She did this with the help and support of the Lord above. My mother was a true Christian woman who loved everyone.

William F. Parker

<u>My dad</u>

My dad was from the old school, so to speak, and did not take any crap. He was an authoritarian and had many of the old timers' attitudes. You know, like, "Children should be seen and not heard." When I asked "Why?" the response was, "Because I said so that's why!" I think that he interpreted me asking why as a challenge. I was just a curious kid who asked a lot of questions that sometimes made him mad.

My dad had a temper and would say mean and hurtful things to us. He would also become physical with us. He used a belt until we were about nine years old. He began using his hands (getting backhanded in the face) and fists thereafter.

I became so angry to where it became a love-hate relationship. I began running away when I was about seven. I'd hide and sleep in an underground garage right down the street from the house. I hid under the cars and would hope that I heard someone before they started their car to go to work. I would roll out from underneath the car before they pulled their car out. Kind of dumb wouldn't you say? I found out years later, that while I was doing that, my brother would go to a neighbor's and would lie with their dog. He would spend time in the doghouse until things at home cooled down before he would return.

I remember my middle brother (who is about 16 months older than I) and I, retreating to the closet and holding each other tightly when we heard the rocks crackling below from dad's car tires in the driveway. That uncomfortable noise meant that dad was home. We cringed and clung to each other because we didn't know if we would be hugged and kissed or smacked in the mouth and knocked across the room when he entered the door.

I remember early on, when it was the belt. First, it was not a measly belt like the things that fall apart in a few months like they do today. He had a thick leather belt that was made for wear and tear. He would have us pull our pants down and hit us the number of times he thought we deserved. The worse the crime, the more whips of the belt. At different times, I had big welts on my back, legs and buttocks. When this happened, you could count on my parents having a big argument because my mother would be infuriated. She would tell him what we all knew. That he had an uncontrollable temper and was too violent with his kids. Most, if not all, arguments my parents had were about their kids. As with many families, dad thought that mom was too soft and let us get away with everything. Mom thought that dad was too strict and in fact abusive.

Sometimes, we were disciplined for some stupid reason like not finishing the food on our plate. Of course, that was not as stupid as I once thought because dad and grandma lived through the Great Depression when food was scarce. They were anything but wasteful and insisted on beating that into us if they had to. You don't understand this when you are a kid.

We may not have cleaned our room nor done the dishes, as he had told us. Don't get me wrong, we were far from angels. We were arguing and fighting all the time. When dad got home and heard from grandma that we weren't listening or that we were fighting with each other all day, he would remind us who the boss was and when he says something, he means it. Grammy was in her 60s when she moved in with us, and when we got her upset, that did not sit well with my father and rightfully so.

Unlike my brothers, I got to a point where I fought back. I would hear stuff like, "You are in my house where I pay the bills, so you will do what I tell you". I would tell him that just because he paid the bills it didn't give him the right to hurt me with his mouth or his hands. That could and often would make him even angrier. If I would have just kept my mouth shut, it would have been better, but good luck with that.

I was a slow learner and that proved painful and costly on many occasions. I remember grabbing his hand as he punched me and biting it. I tried to bite his hand off so he couldn't hit me anymore but that didn't work. That made him even angrier and the beating was worse.

I remember an incident when we were in the car, and dad was taking us back from a state park where we often went to swim. My brother had said something that he didn't like. None of us were old enough to drive at the time, so dad was doing the driving. Without looking back, he swung his arm full force and backhanded me in the face. It was meant for my brother who was sitting next to me.

I yelled and screamed at him and told him that he was an out-of-control maniac. He got quiet because he knew that he was wrong, but he was one of those people who would not apologize. The rest of the ride home was quiet. When we got there, I sat in my room, mad and bitter as hell.

He came to my room a couple of hours later and asked if I wanted to take a ride with him to get tennis shoes. I had told him I needed new ones because those I had were in bad condition. I knew that this was his way of apologizing. I would usually accept because I thought that if I am going to get abused physically or mentally, I earned what he was offering.

This day was different. I told him, "I don't want the damn tennis shoes! I want an apology and to hell with the tennis shoes." So, rather than apologize he said, "To hell with you then you little brat." and stormed out of my room.

With the arguing and fighting came a great deal of resentment and hostility. As I got older, I stayed out of the house so I could avoid the arguments and fights. That's also why the outdoors and sports were my outlets. I played and played and played. I tried to stay away from the house as much as possible.

I came home for dinner (which we all had together until our teen years). Grandma always had a great dinner waiting. Food was often the way love was expressed in our family, like many others I'm sure. That may also explain why I am overweight these days.

To this day, I believe that most of the arguing in our home was because my two brothers and I were subconsciously competing for our father's love. A lot of that probably came from him saying several times a year, "You are no longer my son, and I disown you." That was until the next week, when one of my other brothers was disowned for doing something wrong, and I was back on his good side. To this day, I can remember how much that hurt.

Eventually, it no longer evoked hurt and sadness but anger and disgust. As I got older, I would tell him that he needed to stop saying that because it was just plain mean. He would disown me now, but only until one of my brothers did something wrong, and I was sick of hearing it.

As mentioned earlier, I have had a long history of depression and have attempted suicide many times over the years. I thought that the world would be a better place without me. I felt that I was a burden to my family and the rest of the world. After all, my own father wanted to disown me and no longer claim me as his son, so I must not be worth much.

Being disowned is only a fraction of the things that were said over the years. I also heard that I was a piece of shit and would never do anything with my life. After all, I had epilepsy and was disabled. I was stupid and in special education and did poorly in school. Maybe he was right. Maybe I was right? Maybe the world would be a better place without me.

I cannot remember the precipitating event, but I was so angry at my father for something he said or did and decided that I had had enough. I was nine years old and thought that it was time to bring an end to all the hell for all of us. Grandma was out shopping, and I was home alone. Dad was working and my brothers were out doing whatever. I knew dad had several pistols in his room, and I was desperate to end my pain. I figured that I had tried everything and was still miserable. The only way I could find relief was if I killed myself.

I walked into his room and to the right was his dresser. On the left were his bed and a table that sat next to it. I did not see his snub-nose, 38-caliber pistol that sometimes sat on his dresser. It's called a snub-nose because it has little to no barrel. Subsequently, the farther away the target, the less accurate the shot will be. That wouldn't be a factor because I was going to shoot myself in the head or stick the gun in my mouth and pull the trigger.

Sometimes, he kept it in the top drawer of the table next to his bed. I opened the drawer, and there it was. I grabbed it from the drawer and examined it, as I sat on the side of his bed. I looked at the wooden handle and butt of the gun. I grabbed it more firmly with my left hand and sat the top of the gun and the chamber in my right hand. I looked to confirm that the chamber was full of bullets, that the gun was loaded. The steel was cold. I found it interesting that the gun was almost as cold as dad was.

No wonder he has guns and is good with them. These things hurt and injure like he does. Neither he nor his gun is capable of feeling or apologizing for the damage they do. Then, I also thought about all the things I admired him for, and how much I loved him.

I gripped the gun and began to lift it toward my head. The closer the gun got to my head the warmer my face got. The tears streamed down my cheeks. The gun seemed to get heavier and heavier the closer it got to my head. The anger toward my father and everyone else made me sad. The thoughts and feelings built up in my mind, and my heart began to race. I pulled the gun back down, looked at it and tried to raise it back to my head and couldn't. I began sobbing. I opened the top drawer of the table, threw the gun in the desk and slammed the drawer. I screamed at the top of my lungs in rage because I couldn't do it and would have to continue to live.

I thought about the mess there would have been had I pulled the trigger. Then I thought about the number of different ways that dad might react when he got home from work and walked in his room. Would he be upset with me because of the mess I left? Would he think, well, at least I don't have to deal with his bullshit anymore? Or, would he feel bad for the pitiful, hurt, depressed and self-loathing child that he helped to create?

I wasn't sure then, and I am still not sure today how he would have reacted. For years, I have told people that if I could have awakened for a moment to see his response, I would have pulled the trigger. This was assuming that he would have felt bad for things he did to me. I also think that maybe God made that gun heavier and heavier as I raised it because He knew that this complex and troubled relationship would someday not only come to a truce, but would actually be a close father-son relationship. One that I would cherish before he died.

I do not, for a second, want to paint this terrible picture of my father because he did a lot of commendable things as well. He took us in when my mother couldn't take care of us anymore. He also asked his mother to compromise her health by taking care of him and his three children when she was 60-plus years old.

Dad was very affectionate too. He would hug and kiss us and would allow us to sit on his lap as we watched Mannix or Chiller Theatre, GunSmoke or Bonanza. Dad took us places too. We went to Lake Erie, Conneaut Lake, Disney World, Canada and to see relatives in Kentucky. We went to the Holiday House, which was an entertainment place with dinner, drinks and famous people who would perform. I often fell asleep before the show was over, but it was great because I was with my dad and apparently, on good terms, at least at that time.

We had our private moments as well, that were special. He would ask me to shine his shoes, his police badges and the gold bars that went on top of the shoulders of his shirt because of his rank as a Lieutenant. He put his shirt on, and the badge and bars would shine. He would tuck in his tailored, crisp white shirt into his navy blue pants. He would then put that thick belt on that I had become too familiar with. He slid the belt through the loops until the next to the last one. He would slide his belt through the holster that was holding, sometimes, his 357 magnum, his 9-millimeter or his 38-caliber pistol.

He would finish sliding his belt through the last two loops and then fasten and tighten the buckle. He then put his blackjack in his pants, on his right hip, with it sticking out for quick access, if needed. Dad was right-handed but would put the gun backwards on his left hip. On one of his more patient days, I asked why, and he explained that he did it for two reasons.

One, he could get the gun out faster because it had a 6.5-inch barrel. It would be difficult getting that out of the holster if it were on his right hip. The second reason was, on the right hip like most wear it, someone can come from behind and take it from his holster with ease. However, the way he chose to wear it, it could only be taken out by someone who was facing him. He felt much better about those odds.

The final step was his white hat that also had a badge on the front of it, just above the brim. I would watch him dress for work and be such a proud little boy. Remembering this now, I can't help but have a smile on my face and even a little tear. That is what made things so difficult. The same man, whom I idolized and admired, I sometimes hated.

We had many other private moments that were very special. My father and his friend would drive to Florida almost every year for a 5- or 6-year period. One of those times, he chose to take me with him. There were things that my dad and his friend did on a regular basis when they went there. They liked going to shows and clubs where there were friends that they had come to know over the years.

Dad made sure that he put time aside to spend with me on the beach, walking, talking and swimming. He also took me to places common for tourists. He took me to a place where Jai Alai was played and bet on, like the dog track or horses are here. It was nothing that I would be interested in playing, but it was cool to watch the skilled pros playing it. I didn't care what we did. I was in Florida with my father, and I would have enjoyed almost anything. For two weeks, dad and I got along, and there were no arguments.

When we grew older, my brothers were working or doing something with their friends, and I would be in my little apartment, bored and broke, with nothing to do. Dad would pick me up and take me for rides on his motorcycle or in his car out to the country. Just some time to get away from the city and be in touch with nature and scenery. I too loved scenery and getting away from the city, occasionally. We had that in common for sure. He would stop at a family-owned farm that served bison burgers that had a little store next to it.

Then, there were the regular things that he did, that many kids take for granted but I didn't. I appreciated every moment. He took us swimming, ice skating and out to eat on a pretty regular basis. He, by no means, spoiled us, but we did not go without. When we needed shoes, clothes or anything else, dad took us to the mall and bought it for us. He would stop at a restaurant and buy lunch or dinner for all of us. Sometimes we went for ice cream.

The family spent weekends at Lake Erie, Conneaut Lake Park, Kennywood Park, Schenley and Frick Parks that were in our neighborhood. We were either swimming, learning to fish, ice skating, catching a hardball or softball, shooting baskets, going to the movies, drive-in theatres and more. When we had plans to go fishing, I remember waiting until it got dark. Dad would give us all a flashlight. We would go out in the backyard and behind the garage and search for nightcrawlers.

My favorite adventure might have been after my father had bought one of the police bikes that he rode as a motorcycle cop. He bought it with the sidecar and painted it candy apple red with glitter. I remember the complete joy and pride I had while sitting in the sidecar as dad drove me around our neighborhood. I was about seven years old. It was the coolest thing and for the first time, I could remember that friends envied me. They would say stuff like "Your dad is so cool!" "I wish I could do that with my dad."

So, by no means was it all bad. I think in many ways I had a great dad who was very active in his kids' lives and was always there. I remember how loved and safe I felt when he would give me a big bear hug. He'd wrap his big arms around me and pull me into his fifty-inch chest. The same man who terrified me made me feel safer than anyone on earth.

Then, the day that everyone dreads had arrived. Dad was in his mid-late fifties when he was diagnosed with Lymphoma Cancer. I am not well informed about cancer. I know that just the word itself can strike fear into anyone. I remember dad handling the news reasonably well. The surprise of the diagnosis is what threw us more than anything. After all, dad hardly ever got sick. He did not believe in going to the hospital unless a person was just short of dying. The big C was shocking and scary news, and he knew that he couldn't avoid the hospital or treatment.

Dad was in and out of remission several times, over a six- or seven-year period, and was treated with chemotherapy and radiation. I also remember how weak it made him. Dad didn't have to struggle with hair loss because he didn't have much to begin with.

133

He was a large man who stood about six feet two inches tall and his weight fluctuated between 240 and 260 pounds for most of the 30 years I had known him. He had a belly like many cops, but it was hard as a rock. As he would say, "I have legs like a racehorse." His calves were like steel plates. His thigh muscles were impressive and noticeable, particularly for a guy in his fifties and sixties. He had an athletic 30 years old's legs that held and balanced a policeman's stomach until he retired at fifty-three years of age.

This meant that my dad was only in retirement for about five years before getting the news. Through-out his life, however, he was very active and loved going places and doing things. Naturally, the radiation and chemotherapy weakened him and restricted his activity. You could see that this bothered him a great deal. Although he was weak, he insisted on going for walks. I would show up at the house and walk with him. Periodically, he would have to sit down on a neighbor's steps or a wall in front of their house. At some point, I would have to put his arm around my neck and bear his weight and help him to balance until we made it back home.

There are life changing moments that occur when we least expect them, and this was one of them. We were taking our usual walk around the block. I took his arm from around my neck as we both sat to rest. He looked me dead in my eyes and said, "Son, since all of this has happened, you have been my rock. You have helped me through all of this, and I can't tell you what that means to me." I began to tear up and gave him the biggest hug.

Though there were other times when dad had complimented me or said something kind, this was the moment when I was finally where I wanted to be. I now was part of his heart and felt truly loved and accepted by him. I felt genuinely appreciated like no other time in my life. I was on a cloud following that talk while resting on a neighbor's steps.

Many times, since his passing in 1992, I have felt unappreciated as I'm sure we all do. So, what do I do when I need a boost? I go back to that moment in my life and get the boost I need to move forward and not get stuck feeling sorry for myself. Just as dad's negative comments were powerful, so too were his positive comments and particularly this one.

Our relationship continued to improve more and more over the years. I tried to be there for him as often as I could. I tried to be less of a burden to him by improving myself and my life. Yes, I was still drinking, but I began to decrease my usage. When I was drunk, I stayed away until I was sober and level-headed. I did not want my father to have any more pressure or stress than what he was already dealing with. I wanted him to have the best chance possible in overcoming cancer and upsetting him would not help him to do that.

I had stopped smoking for a couple of years following my lung surgery, and dad was very happy about that. Therefore, I did not let him know that as his health got progressively worse, I started smoking again. In the last several weeks of his life, I consumed a lot of gum and mints so he could not smell the smoke on my breath.

Every time I had a cigarette, I went into the bathroom and washed my hands before returning to his hospital room. He may have been suspicious just because I smelled so good every time I returned to his room, but he never said anything either way.

For the last six weeks of my father's life, I stayed with dad in his hospital room and slept on a cot. I was in my first semester at our local community college and was taking 14 credits. After a full day of classes, I would take a bus back to the hospital to take care of my dad in the evening. I studied every night as I watched him sleep. On the other hand, I often fell asleep while studying. I would wake up startled because the pencil I was writing with fell from my grip and hit the table.

When I study, I try to become as focused as possible, because I know that I must fight my ADHD. Without realizing it, I guess I had developed a routine. When I had a break in concentration, I would look over at dad to see if he was okay, and then I would look at the heart monitor.

I would feed him when the meals arrived, and sometimes bathe him as he lay in bed, weak and incapable of doing so himself. It was not easy watching my father deteriorate a little more every day. He began whining as he used to accuse me of, and said he just wanted to go because he had lived a full life and didn't want to deal with it anymore.

A burst of anger went through me. I guess it was the hostility I still had from the many mean things he had said to me over the years when I complained about how bad my life was, and all the struggles I was going through. I figured that now it was my turn to tell him like it is. I leaned over his bed, looked him in the eyes and reminded him of the years and years we heard that we were quitters, losers and would never amount to anything. I told him that he was not sounding like the big shot cop he used to be but more like a coward.

I went on to tell him that all of this wasn't just about him and that he owed it to himself and to all of us that loved him, to make his best effort to stay alive. I told him that his son, (me) who was trying to go to college (when I knew damn well, he wasn't smart enough to finish) and then come back every day to take care of him and he was going to give up! Really?

In one respect, I understood because by now, he had been complaining for a while about needing his fingers pricked several times a day to keep track of his blood levels for all different stuff including diabetes, liver problems and many other things. He had been taken for testing over several weeks, getting all kinds of things done.

I understood what he was going through. Not because I ever had cancer, but because of all the time I had spent in the hospital by then, which was far more than he had. I had the spinal taps, angiograms, EEGs, EKGs and PET scans. This doesn't include all the accidents and injuries from having severe seizures. It doesn't include the numerous ER visits from being a drunk, being attacked in the street and almost getting killed.

On the other hand, this was not the courageous father who served in WWII and went to work and put his life on the line every day for over 30 years. I was so upset and disgusted. I told him to think about what I just said, and that I would be back. I guess it was out of spite, because I also told him that I was going to a nearby bar to drink and catch a buzz, and there wasn't a thing he could do about it.

When I returned from the bar, I had done just what I told him and that was to catch a buzz. My disgust wasn't gone but now it was directed toward me for talking to him like that. I was upset at using our argument as an excuse to have about six mixed drinks and smoke about ten cigarettes in the two hours I was gone.

But when I returned something magical happened. Instead of dad submitting to the cancer and giving up, he submitted to me. Really? Was something wrong with my hearing? He said something like, Jeff you are right! Over the last couple of hours, I have thought about what you said, and I realize what a real baby I have sounded like with all the complaining and whining that I have been doing. I couldn't believe what I was hearing. I began to wonder if someone had put something in my drink.

Then, for the first time in my life, my father apologized to me. He said, I also want to apologize to you because I now realize the hell you went through as a little boy. I thought about all of the spinal taps you had beginning when you were just 3 or 4 years old. I thought about all of your injuries and neurological testing and all of the times you were in the hospital for the seizures, and I was not there for you like I should have been.

Dad said that he did not know how much more he had in him to fight but promised me that he would give it everything he had. I went over and put my cheek against his and hugged him as I sobbed. I thanked him for considering what I had said and that was the dad I had always known. He was a man with courage, who would give it his best shot. There was a catch though. He asked me to promise him that I would not drop out of community college and would do everything in my power to be the first in my family to get a college degree.

Because dad was not someone to get caught up in emotions, he tried to break the seriousness and intimacy of that moment with humor. With a big smile on his face he said, "Thanks for telling my ass off. I needed it". We both smiled and chuckled.

Dad fought hard for about two or three more weeks after that and was showing great improvement. All of us were becoming more hopeful. Shortly thereafter, he lost all his strength. He looked at me and said, "I just can't anymore. I don't have anything left to fight." I looked at him with tears in my eyes and told him that he fought the good fight, and now, I just wanted him to let me take care of him and make him as comfortable as possible the rest of the way.

I think it was late afternoon, early evening on May 5, 1992. I was studying as usual but was looking more and more frequently at the heart machine as his heart rate went slower and slower. I knew it wasn't long before it would be over, so I called all our family members and a couple of family friends who wanted to be there with him.

Everyone who wanted to be there was standing around his bed telling him how much he was loved and would be missed. Though I never thought I would see it anywhere other than on TV, the moment came when the heart machine flat-lined and that horrible and irritating high-pitched sound continued until the medical staff came in to turn it off.

His many different battles were over, and by God's grace ours were too. Dad and I had become the best of friends over the last several years of his life. He never saw me graduate from college, but he saw me working on it, and he was proud. Like Archie Bunker, dad had a big heart and could feel. He just hid it well. He was able to let me see that side of him when he knew that he was not going to be here any longer and for that I am grateful.

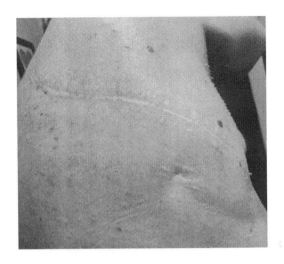

Section I, Collapsed Lung

Lung surgery was required and a pneumothorax (fluid was drained from my lung)

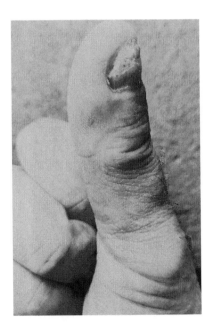

Section I, Louisville Slugger

Crushed thumb from covering my head as I was being beat in the head with a baseball bat.

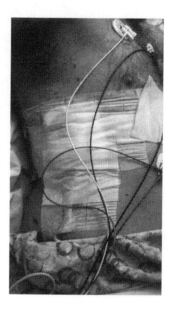

Section I, New Material for the book

Seven ribs broken in ten places after falling twenty feet from my porch. Had a hemothorax and a tube was used to drain blood from building around my lung

Section I, New material for the book.
This is the view from where I fell.

Section II, From incorrigible to Institutionalized
My dear mother and I in 1971 when I was in McIntyre Shelter.

Section II, From Incorrigible to Institutionalized
Graduation after getting my GED at New Castle Youth
Development Center

Section III, Family
The Parker Brothers in 1964. I was two years old.

Section III, Family
Jeff and Gregg

Section III, Family
Dad and Jeff in the mid 1970's

Section III, Family
Dad and Jeff in the mid 1970's

Section III, Family

Lieutenant Parker. My dad was the youngest officer ever (at the time) to be promoted to Lieutenant at the young age of thirty six or thirty seven which he obviously wasn't in this picture.

Section III, Family

Me visiting my mom as she stayed in long-term care.

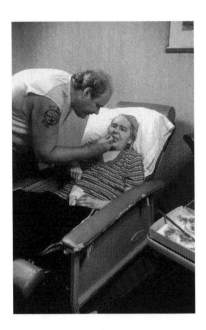

Section III
Mom and I in 2016.

Section III, Family
My brother Lance. A gifted sax player.

Section III, Family

Lance and Jeff after a great performance. I love hearing my bother make that horn do magic

Section IV Moving on Up

Community College of Allegheny County 1992-1995, AS in Criminal Justice.

Section IV, Moving on Up
The University of Pittsburgh, Cathedral of Learning. 1997 BASW, 1998 MSW.

Section III Family
Vicki helps us make a snowman

Section III Family
Jeff bonding with his nineteen year old cat, Domino

Section III Family
Prince and Buddy are BFFs

Section III Family
Kim and I going formal

Section III Family
With the woman I love on a beautiful Summer afternoon at Frick Park.

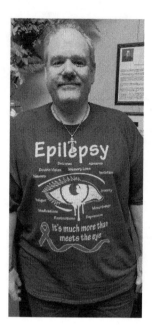

Advocacy
Epilepsy is a cause that is near and dear to my heart.

Advocacy
Celebrating Recovery every year in the City of Pittsburgh.

Advocacy

I will keep fighting to help people find recovery from opioid addction.

SECTION IV

Moving ON UP

"<u>Education is Power</u>." This is not to take away from the man-made millionaires or those who have well-paying jobs that don't require a college degree. However, many things have become specialized and training or certification is usually needed. Whether it is an actual diploma or becoming certified in a vocational or technical trade also known as vo-tech, that piece of paper has become a critical factor in proving competency and landing a good job with benefits.

There are times in our lives that, if we look back, we can see how one decision changed the course of our life. Had we chosen differently, we would likely have had an entirely different life. For example, I chose to have the police officer who caught me for the umpteenth time absconding from home take me to an institution instead of returning me to my home. After all, that decision resulted in seven years of being transferred from one institution to another. Many terrible experiences occurred during those years, and they changed me. I was not part of my family for a long time, and the list goes on and on.

Things might have been worse had I stayed at home, but I will never know. However, you can see the point I am making. The decision made that one evening changed my life and my world. There are also good things that can come from making an important decision at a crucial time in life. One of them was enrolling in college at Community College of Allegheny County.

Community College of Allegheny County

This decision put me on a path toward normalcy. Going to CCAC was the starting point of a new life. However, deep down, I didn't believe that I had what it took to complete the two-year program. In fact, it took me three years to get my two-year degree. I knew the problems that I had in school when I was younger, due to my ADHD diagnosis. I knew the damage my years of smoking marijuana, getting drunk and the neurological problems from the epilepsy had caused in my early education. The many head injuries I had sustained over the years could all hinder my efforts to earn a degree.

I was going to have to read, concentrate, comprehend and memorize information. This meant I would have to utilize my damaged brain. I knew that I had always been a pretty good athlete and excelled in the past, but academia, not so much. I was not confident to say the least and for good reasons.

I knew the odds were against me but that was nothing new, especially when it came to school. I thought that I was too old to be going back to school at the ripe age of thirty. I remember someone telling me that if I waited ten years to enroll, I would be forty so, do it now. Hmmm? Interesting logic. That was not part of my psyche at that time. I came to find that the average age of students was twenty-eight or twenty-nine years old back then.

I was on disability for many years for clinical depression, epilepsy, alcoholism and PTSD. This made me eligible for grant money to help pay my tuition. Being an older student, in addition to the above factors, would categorize me as an atypical student. Many of these factors made me eligible for the ACT 101 program at CCAC. The ACT 101 program was created by the late K. Leroy Irvis. He was the first African American speaker of the House of Representatives for the state of Pennsylvania. He represented the City of Pittsburgh and was an advocate for higher education.

An article in the Pittsburgh Post-Gazette (February 9, 2016) entitled, "Remembering the Lion of Pennsylvania", explained that this man was "the lead author on legislation that created the Pennsylvania Higher Education Assistance Agency." This agency is known as

PHEAA. It provided a significant amount of grant money to pay for my education at CCAC. There are more than 70 schools in the state of Pennsylvania that have ACT 101 programs, and all of us who are and were beneficiaries of these resources owe the late K. Leroy Irvis a great deal of thanks for his dedication to education. He helped many of us to earn a college degree and without this assistance, we would never have been able to consider going to college.

In addition to the grant money, the CCAC ACT 101 program provides many other services which I needed and utilized during my time there. The program had a counselor, the late Thomas Canada, who I grew to respect and love for the support he provided me during my time there. He and I became friends, following my time there, and we stayed in touch over the years. In fact, Mr. Canada and I had talked within a week or two of his demise.

Ann Tanski was a tutor early on, who eventually became the Director of the ACT 101 program. She and I spent a lot of time together because I certainly needed the help from tutoring services. This program was the reason I was able to graduate. I am convinced that had I begun at a major college, I would never have graduated from college. College and education were like a maze to me, and I was lost. The program and those working in it, almost literally, held my hand to guide me and assist me until I could get around myself. It was like the training wheels that are needed when a child begins to ride a bike. At some point, the training wheels come off and the parent lets go, and you are on your own.

Studying, learning and being productive in school were things that I was never good at. In addition, my father died in my first semester of school at CCAC. The trial for the aggravated assault charges was just ahead, and I could be going to prison anyhow. I was thinking about quitting early on, and more specifically, was going to use my father's death as an excuse to withdraw from school.

Thomas Canada told me that he would not allow me to quit, and in fact, he would come to my house and pick me up to make sure that I made it to school every day because I had too much to offer the world and could not do that if I dropped out. He insisted that I was going to become a good student because he had seen how hard I was trying, and how much effort I was making to be a good student. He insisted that if I continued to work hard and not give up, he was sure that I would graduate with honors. Strangely enough, he was right.

The challenges were endless. In addition to the emotional strain from dad's death and the anxiety and worry about the upcoming trial, I was still drinking. People who are addicted to drugs or alcohol are strategists. We find a way of doing things and getting them done despite trying to make it as difficult as possible. For example, I wanted the best of both worlds, to be able to study and drink, so this is what I did. I'd get off the bus at the bar I frequented with my bookbag. When I showed up, the bartender who knew me (like a book) would give me, not just a draft beer, but a full pitcher of beer and a full glass of beer without my even having to order it.

I would get a table that was away from the bar and others and get the book out. I would begin reading and highlighting the important stuff. I would consume about three pitchers of beer while reading and highlighting a few chapters until the words on the page would begin to blur. This was a hint that studying time was over, and it was time to party. It was then, that I put my college stuff away, went over to the bar, and began doing shots of whiskey and shooting pool. I'd wake up with a hangover at 6 am to take two buses to make it to my morning classes.

Thomas Canada is one of the reasons that I have a different life today. As mentioned earlier, his conversation with me was another life-changing time. If I had dropped out as I had been considering, I would never have earned any of my college degrees and the many amazing things that have come from this would never have happened. More than likely I would be dead by now. Because of Thomas Canada, Ann Tanski and my hard work, I was able to become a regular Dean's List student at CCAC.

When Ann Tanski was promoted to Director of the ACT 101 program, she asked me if I was interested in becoming an Advisory Board Member of the program. I felt honored and accepted her offer. I was invited regularly as a guest speaker for the pre-college students.

This is just one of the endless examples of how things had taken a 180 degree turn. I went from being a student who was part of this wonderful program to an advisory board member of this same program.

When I came as a guest speaker and talked to the pre-college students, I saw the same lack of confidence on their faces that I had felt for years. It excited me to spread the word about the great work that the ACT did for you even if your abilities are limited. I told them that through hard work, motivation and perseverance, they could benefit if they did their part with dedication. This was a successful formula that would enable them to succeed despite any flaws they might have.

I like the old expression, "God has a sense of humor." I became addicted to learning and the more I learned the hungrier I became for more information. I became well known in the library at CCAC because I would spend three to as many as five hours a day there. Fellow students asked me if I owned the cubicle I nearly lived in or was I still renting or leasing it?

I had never been an honor roll student, prior to college, and barely passed my GED test but I was becoming pretty good at it and even more amazingly, I loved it. I found the campus to be exhilarating and as my focus on studies increased, my time drinking decreased and therefore, I drank less and less. I was at CCAC from 1992-1995 and had three or four courses in my final semester at CCAC. For the first time in my life, I got straight As. To some reading this, it may not be that big of a deal but to me, a miracle had just happened. I graduated with a 3.42 GPA and earned an AS in Corrections Administration. My initial plans were to become a Probation Officer, but I changed my mind.

I had heard that many of the POs were now armed, and this wasn't something I wanted to do. To begin with, I was not my father. If I wanted to carry a gun, I would have gone in my father's footsteps and become a cop. I'm sure that my past would have been a hindrance, and I had enough of that. I had kept my promise to my father and had graduated from college. The bad part was that he was no longer here to see it. For this reason, any of the milestones I have had since his passing have been bitter-sweet.

The great part is that there are many who were still here to see it, most importantly, my mother! I was able to show her that her love and tolerance and unconditional love had paid off as she had always said it would.

When I graduated, I had the confidence to take the next step and write a letter to the Assistant Dean at the University of Pittsburgh's School of Social Work to explain why I should be accepted there. I received a return letter saying that I had been accepted. Similar feelings were evoked as when I began at CCAC. I was filled with joy and terror, and I'm not sure of which there was more.

I immediately began questioning if I could do this. Was I even capable of earning a Bachelor's Degree or was that too high a level of education? I couldn't imagine another being able to achieve such a goal. Then I began to think, well that's what you thought about CCAC, and you graduated with honors. I remembered what the owner of the bar told me one day. He said, "Even if you fail you will be where you are right now, but you won't know, if you don't try it." I also remembered the part about the free drinks there for the whole weekend if I failed, but I doubted that the same deal was on the table three years later. Though I was still drinking and continued for a few more years, it was no longer a priority in my life or a goal to do every day because I was in withdrawal.

The most encouraging factors were people like Terry Barnes, (who was kind enough to give his input about me in this book), and a couple of others with whom I had been at CCAC. They, too, had transferred to "Pitt". I would see them regularly, and we were in some of the same classes together. Despite this, I still was not sure that I could do it and was plain scared when I began. The early classes had 50-100 or more students and that was intimidating, but as usual, I got through it.

I chose Social Work as my major at Pitt because it is such a wide-open field and social workers can and do so many different things. This would provide many different employment opportunities if I managed to graduate. I was also told that at that time, the School of Social Work at Pitt was well respected and the Bachelor program was ranked fifth in the country. It was one bus away from where I was living, so that didn't hurt.

As you can see, familiarity was key for me. Some get excited about leaving home to go to school but not me. Another important reason for choosing Pitt was that my grandmother was in her 90s. I wanted to be close to home so that I could see her and spend time with her before she passed away, which happened not long after I began attending classes there.

I quickly learned why the school was ranked so high. The studies were grueling, and the expectations were high for the students. I had become a better reader while at CCAC. That was crucial because I remember reading between three hundred to six hundred pages a week. I know people who are avid readers and read a book a day, but I am not one of them.

The challenges seemed endless. Of course, I did not have my own computer at the time, and so I had to use those at the Hillman Library on campus or the computer system at the school. I am not a computer person, so it would take me nearly a semester to get used to the software/ programs they had. Just when I did, they would change something, and it would take me nearly another semester to get used to those changes. Thank goodness for the help and assistance provided at the Hillman Library because without them, I doubt that I would have graduated.

The possibility of getting my degree at Pitt became more and more real every day. I would turn in assignments and see an A, A- or a B for my grade in nearly every course I had. Many of the things that I had seen only in my imagination, when I was waking up with hangovers and living in my dark world, were now coming to fruition.

When I was getting drunk every day and going in and out of the hospital and in and out of jail, I would see childhood friends periodically, and ask them what they had been doing. They would say, "I have been busy at school and studying a lot." A few years later, I would see them and hear, "I've been buried in my books, and I'm in law school now." I would imagine what it must be like to live the college life. I knew that the only way that I would experience it would be through my imagination.

After all, I'm an epileptic drunk with ADHD who was in special education because I was slow. I began to think differently. I began thinking that "Wow, this is the real thing". I am in college, and I am not just passing my classes but doing so with pretty darn good grades. I would also remember the expression, "God has a sense of humor." He must, when the same person who was a poor reader and didn't like to read chose a major that would require three hundred to six hundred pages of reading a week and liked it. It became even more real when I began my practicums/internships and would work at different agencies as part of my studies and training for experience in the field. Most importantly, I liked it and was told that I was pretty good at it.

I attended every graduation and every outing for graduates possible. I wanted to have the same unforgettable experiences my childhood friends had had about fifteen years earlier and ingest it all. CCAC and Pitt were similar in that community college had a graduation celebration for the ACT 101 Program on campus and then another for the entire school at the David Lawrence Convention Center. Pitt's School of Social Work had one graduation ceremony at the Soldiers and Sailors facility on campus, and the entire University's ceremony was at the old Civic Arena that no longer exists.

It seems like there was always a fear factor when I had reached a milestone and was ready to begin working on the next. When I decided to stay at Pitt to earn my Master's Degree, I received a letter telling me that because I now had a Bachelor's Degree, I could not be disabled anymore and would no longer get my monthly check that I had been getting for so many years due to my clinical depression, alcoholism and epilepsy. That meant that I would not have a job or a check to pay my rent.

What was I going to do? Here I am in my mid-thirties, and I have no real work experience. I have been on disability all my life, and I am now being told that I will no longer be receiving a check. Don't misunderstand! I was most grateful for every dime that had been given to me over the years. The fear was that I would not have a job yet or income despite being a college graduate. This was all new to me and was very frightening.

The same friends who had gone to college had also talked about their tuition payments that they had to make, at least those who were not having their parents pay for their education. Because I was beginning to feel a little more normal and like a real part of society, instead of someone with a limited life in the subculture of addiction, I decided to get a loan that would cover my tuition and my expenses and pay my bills. This was a scary move but one that had to be made.

As I had at CCAC and the Bachelor's program, I did very well in the graduate program and earned my Master's Degree in the field of Social Work in 1998. I was not able to become employed until six months later. My loan money was almost gone when I was hired for my first real job. It was then, that the fear set in yet again. I had stopped drinking for about a year when I got my first job out of college, and I was seizure-free for a brief period as well.

I was overwhelmed with fear. What would happen if I started having seizures again? Could or would I lose my job? Would I be able to get back on a fixed income or be homeless and hungry with a Master's Degree? What if I was a drunk again? Could I handle the responsibility of the job? What if I became depressed and suicidal again? If even one of these things happened, how would I pay back my loans?

The fact is, these thoughts came in a very short time and rather than be haunted by them, I shut them out and began thinking things like, am I crazy? I went to school for seven years to better my life and get off a fixed income (SSI). Now I'm going to worry about going to work when that is what I have been striving for all this time? I remember that I didn't think that I could do any of this and have done it. I told myself to shut up, go to work and be grateful. You will have a steady income and medical insurance because you went to school for so long. I put my tie and blazer on and left for work. I didn't have a car or driver's license until years later, so I got on the bus and went to work like everyone else did in my new world.

I assume that most, if not all of us, are a little uncomfortable when we start a new job but manage to adjust. I did too. Where it was different was, I was thirty-six years old before I got my first real, career job where taxes were taken out of my check, and I had third-party insurance that helped pay for my medications and other medical care instead of the government.

I found out rather quickly that I had chosen the right field and liked it a lot. I couldn't believe that I was now getting paid to work with people with problems like mental health and addiction and was working and involved with the criminal justice system. Heck, I was at home. Only now, I was on the other side of the desk, and in a position to help people struggling with the same things that I had. It doesn't get much more humbling, honorable and gratifying than that.

I have heard over the years that "education is power", and my life is an example of that. The moment I enrolled in college, my goals, my life and my experiences began to expand outside of the subculture of addiction and being "disabled." Education enabled me to see new possibilities that at one time, I could only imagine. Today they are my reality. I will be forever grateful to the ACT 101 program at CCAC, as well as the University of Pittsburgh and the School of Social Work and all of those who helped me along the way. You helped me to achieve my goals so that I could change my world and live a different life.

George Jefferson's Show's Theme Song

I was born in a nice neighborhood but before I knew it, my parents were divorced, and I was living in the projects, and we were poor. I was then rescued by my dad and lived in a nice neighborhood for a few years. This started the process of many years where my address was an agency, an institution or a place that was controlled and subsidized by the county or the state. This explains my first seventeen years.

When I was discharged from my final juvenile institution, I went out on my own, if that's what you want to call it. I wasn't really on my own because through the years, my mother paid frequent visits and would often give me food that she had prepared so that I could have decent meals. The hamburgers and eggs that I was having for breakfast, lunch and dinner weren't going to suffice, and she knew it.

My first place was a room at a large home owned by an old woman. She was kind enough to allow me to stay there and pay a reasonably small amount of my SSI check for rent. Because this was her private home and not an apartment building, she did not have the basics that most take for granted like a bathroom, stove or refrigerator.

To shower, I had to go to a different part of her home and to refrigerate my food I placed it in the box gutter that was arm's length outside of the third story window of the room I was living in. I could not use the stove because it was on the first floor and would impede on the owner's privacy. So I bought a warming pot that could be plugged into the wall to heat my food.

I bought soups and stews in cans that could be stored in bags and once opened the can was put in the box gutter to prevent the food from spoiling. Though her house was very big and very nice, my area was restricted and limited. But I could call this restricted and limited room mine and that's what counted. I didn't want to live with my family members and therefore, these conditions were worth it to me.

After all, I was still resentful as hell toward most, if not all, my family members. The other thing I wanted to do was play ball, get high and drink myself into oblivion. Now I could do all of that without having to hear that I was wasting my life away. Deep down, I knew that was true, but I didn't care much at that time and didn't want to hear about it. "Just leave me alone," I thought, (like most of you have when I was locked up) and let me do my thing.

This setup was for a brief period during the fall and winter months. I inhabited a few other places, and one was worse than the other. One of my apartments had a refrigerator and a stove in it, so in that regard, I was moving on up. The downside was that with these two luxuries, a sink and a stove and my bed, there was barely enough room to stand because the apartment was the size of a jail cell.

There was a bathroom on the same floor, but I had to share it with three other tenants that were often as drunk as I was and were old enough to be my dad. It was in the East Liberty neighborhood, which was becoming more and more dangerous all the time.

I would go to my childhood neighborhood, where family and friends lived to play ball, get drunk and high. Every night was taking a chance of being assaulted, robbed or even killed. I would get a bus and walk home every night. I was often staggering drunk. This made me an easy target to be robbed. The problem was that I had to have money to be robbed. I was attacked a few times while living in this area. The attackers were not happy when they found out that I didn't have any money. They would give me a few more blows to the head before walking away laughing.

My next step was getting an apartment that was in a better and safer neighborhood. It was a basement apartment that I would live in for sixteen and a half years. It was an efficiency apartment. The living room and bedroom were the same place. I had a kitchen and a bathroom of my own though. It was like the Taj Mahal compared to my previous places. My father had talked to a friend, who owned apartment buildings and was able to get me the place.

This building had fourteen units, and I lived in three of them over almost twenty-five years. Well over sixteen of those years were in the basement. When I earned my Master's Degree from Pitt, I saved enough to move to the other side of the building and up to a first-floor apartment. My theme song became *Moving on Up* like the song at the beginning of the old comedy show called "The Jeffersons".

I was now living in a real apartment, working a white-collar job and going to work with a tie and a blazer every day. I was getting a taste of how others lived for the first time in my life, and I was thirty-seven years old. My whole world started to open up and become brighter and brighter, literally and figuratively. When I was living in the basement, about one hour of light would enter my apartment a day. With my new apartment, it was bright all the time. Even on cloudy days, it was brighter than what I was used to.

Even though things were changing for the better it was certainly a period of adjustment. Living above ground helped with my depression. Many of us with depression prefer that our surroundings are dark, and often we keep the curtains closed and the lights dimmed, if not off. I was becoming more normal all the time, because I found myself letting the light in and enjoying it. I was even keeping my place clean and washing dishes.

I began to move up financially as well. One can only move up so much when it comes to social work, but relatively speaking, I am doing well and will always be grateful for the financial assistance I received in the past. I went from paying a monthly rent that consumed nearly half of my income, to a much higher rent in a much nicer apartment that consumed just one third of my income. My living conditions were much better, and I had created some healthy and sober relationships.

Little by little, my life was becoming brighter and brighter. Every day, I am working with sober people with college degrees. Early in my career, I was beginning to see that my life was drastically changing.

When Things Began to Change

Most, if not all of us, can look back and identify life-changing experiences. Something significant happens that shifts things, whether it be our outlook, our motivations and energy, our goals and values or many other things.

With all the experiences that I have shared, you may wonder how so many terrible things can happen, and they weren't significant enough for me to change. The fact is timing is everything. If one is not ready to change, it is not likely to happen. I try to remember that everyone has different tolerance levels for pain, havoc, chaos and stress. What may be a changing moment or experience for one, may not even faze another. That's what makes life so interesting and adventurous.

There is an expression in self-help groups like AA and NA that states, "You have to get sick and tired of being sick and tired". Many of these clichés used in self-help groups are found to be true. I have been asked countless times what the turning point was in my life. What happened that made me want to stop using alcohol and change the course of my life.

I explain that there are a few different things that happened, within a short period of time that helped to turn me in a different direction. One was a legal trial where I was the defendant. I was arrested, and charged with aggravated assault and if convicted, I could have gone to prison for 4-7 years. The other was the death of my father. I remember the trial being postponed, so that I could attend my father's funeral.

It was a sunny afternoon, and I was drinking in the backyard of my apartment building. A friend showed up with a friend of his. They had the liquor and I had the beer, so we drank and drank until all three of us were drunk. Naturally, an argument ensued. I told them that I had had enough, and they could leave. I turned to go back into my apartment building, and while my back was turned, they attacked me.

While on the ground I was kicked in the chin and all 250 pounds of me (at that time) was literally lifted off the ground. My neurosurgeon proved to be as good as I heard because less than a year before this, I had neck surgery, a cervical fusion. I didn't realize that I was not crippled from the kick to the chin until I was running to the front of the building to escape them.

I was reminded that I had a knife in my sweatpants, when I felt it bouncing in the pant leg of my sweats as I ran from them. I got it from my pant leg and one of the guys was in front of me and one was behind, so I could not get into my apartment building. I told the guy in front of me to get out of my way, but he did not. In fact, he lunged toward me. His friend was close behind me when the guy in front of me lunged at me. I swung the knife to keep him away from me, and it contacted his neck.

I ran around him and up the front steps of my apartment building. I looked back. He had fallen into the arms of his friend. I called #911 and the police and paramedics arrived. Although I was the one retreating and was attacked by the two of them first, I was the one arrested. We were both taken to the same hospital. I was taken by the police, and he was taken by the paramedics. The slice from the knife caused him to lose a lot of blood. I needed to have testing to see if my neck was intact. While I was waiting for the test results, I got nearly 40 stitches.

My mother played detective and brought her camera. She took pictures of the scene that showed the drops of my blood from the back of the building to the front, as well as close pictures of the several lacerations on my head and chin that all required stitches. The pictures mom took of the scene of the fight and the medical records would all be presented at the trial.

I remember the judge saying, "I find the defendant, Jeffrey Parker, Not Guilty." He pointed out that there were two of them and one of me, and that it was a predictable incident when alcohol was involved. He stated that I, too, had significant injuries and needed many stitches. He said that the primary reason for the acquittal was because the neck wound was a slice and not a gouge, and to him, this indicated that the defendant was not the aggressor but was trying to fend off his two attackers.

When I heard the judge's words, "NOT GUILTY", I was relieved, emotionally drained and exhausted. The first thing I thought was that finally, something went my way. Things turned out the way they should and justice was served. To date, the system had not been very good or fair to me. I knew that this was not a position I ever wanted to be in again. I knew that to ensure that, I had to begin living a different lifestyle.

I remember another memorable moment that contributed to that turning point. I was drinking in a bar one night, and someone I knew asked me where I thought I would be in life a few years from now. I told him that I wasn't sure that I would be alive tomorrow and you are asking me about a few years from now? I didn't have a clue.

Because of this, I had no plans and therefore no goals. How could I have goals when I don't even know what I want? Over the years, I have kept this in the back of my mind and have seen, if not duplicate, very similar answers from my clients/patients consistently over the years. An estimated 80% or higher seem to have no idea what they want to do with their lives. The fact is you cannot work toward something when you don't know what you want.

It's a given that many college students change their major about 1 ½ - 2 times while in college. But the important part is that they decided to at least go to college. So, it's important to choose a direction and commit to it. For example, my initial choice was criminal justice which is what I got my AS in, while at community college.

I thought that I wanted to become a Probation Officer. However, after hearing that it was not uncommon for a PO to return to a car that had been damaged (spray painted, wheels removed, dented) and God knows what else, I began to question my choice. I had also heard that many POs were choosing to carry a gun. That made the job of a PO sound more like being a cop, and I did not want that. So, I decided to pursue a degree in social work because with that degree there were far more options and subsequently, more job opportunities.

As many of you may have heard, education is power. Well, I can attest to that because prior to going to college, I was dependent on everything and everybody but myself. In the long process of earning my degrees, I learned discipline, commitment to something other than a chemical substance, my family and friends for financial and emotional support not to mention my dependence on the government for SSI, public assistance (welfare), food stamps and medical coverage for testing, medical procedures and nearly 40 years of my medications.

Through the seven years I spent in college, I learned to believe in myself and for that reason, my self-esteem, self-worth and a sense of empowerment developed. Through this process, I learned not only the academic stuff, but more importantly, I learned what I was capable of when I got off my ass and began to work toward specific goals.

Achieving these goals would enable me to depend on myself for my financial security. It was a team effort between me and my employer, to pay for my medical benefits so that I could afford any medical treatments and testing, as well as, my needed medications. I was finally, doing things that others had been doing for many generations, and that many take for granted. I know what it is like to live on the other side of the tracks, and I will never take anything for granted and will appreciate all the things I have, including the little things.

As I continued in school, I learned what it was like to owe money for something other than a ten- or twenty-dollar bill that I borrowed to get a bottle of booze. No, this was the real deal. I am talking about thousands of dollars that are gaining interest until I pay it off. Most of you may not believe this, but I paid what I owed and the interest gladly.

I felt privileged to have the loan, just as I had on my supplemental income, because without it, I could not have gone to school, graduated and earned my credentials. This was not only an investment in my future, but an opportunity to establish credit. By paying it off, a guy who had been receiving welfare checks would be able to buy his own house. Imagine that.

Collecting from welfare, getting SSI and having all my medical expenses paid by the state was the reason I was able to have medications for my seizure disorder, treatment for my mental health problems (inpatient and outpatient) and medications for that as well. I knew that the money I was receiving was a privilege and not a right. I could have been homeless and living on the street all my adult years, but I had a roof over my head and the medications I needed.

I would hear people complaining about having to pay off loans and their taxes. Too many people take things for granted and don't realize that their life can change as soon as they take that first pain pill or take that first drink or gamble their money away. It could change from a natural disaster, a life- threatening medical problem like cancer or become disabled and unable to work or pay the bills any longer. The next thing they know they have lost their house and everything they have ever owned. Therefore, I gladly pay my taxes knowing that this money is going to others who need it and are experiencing hard times as I once did.

Slowly but surely, I began to climb the ladder and life has gotten a little better all the time. Then, a strange thing began to happen. Because I was doing the right things the right way and was working hard to better myself and my life, good things began to snowball. I was taken aback. I initially thought something was wrong because this couldn't be. The only things I ever knew that would snowball were the bad things. Once I realized that I was not delusional and that good stuff snowballing was a reality, I accepted it with open arms and began to see more and more clearly that hard work and education is power and more importantly, empowering.

With this comes increased motivation and responsibility which I welcomed. I must admit that it was a little scary at first but only because it was something new. After all I had been through, I was beginning to see how "normal" people lived life, but I was not taking any of it for granted. Another great change was that I was beginning to see that all the adversities of the past were beginning to look more like blessings. The many years of darkness have made me more insightful about my life and enabled me to appreciate everything that I have internally and externally because I take nothing for granted. It would be a moral crime to act like I have done this all on my own. I have had many people make a difference in my life and help me along the way, some knowingly and others not.

To the strangers like the woman who answered her door at 3 am. She gave me hot coffee and covered me in quilts after I woke up face down in eight inches of snow, passed out from being drunk, thank you. To the woman who stayed with me when I was assaulted and had a collapsed lung and struggled to breathe. You waited until the paramedics came and wished me well, and I thank you for that. For the man who stopped on the dark road and gave me a ride when I had been kidnapped, thank you.

To those I know, like my favorite grade school teacher, Mrs. Silverman, my high school principal, Mr. Bill Fisher, AKA, "The Hook," and all my CCAC professors, particularly Joe DeBlassio, PhD (my lifelong friend since I graduated in 1995), thank you. To my academic advisor, tutor, counselor and friend, Thomas Canada (who passed away while I was writing this book), I give you my thanks. I told Thomas that he was a big part of my being able to graduate as he helped me through my dad's death with support, encouragement and motivation. Ann Tanski, my former tutor who asked me to become an advisory board member of the ACT 101 program for which I was a recipient and benefited from the great things that program did for me when I was a student, thank you.

A thank you goes out to faculty at the University of Pittsburgh, like James Cox, who was my counselor and helped me get through some tough times while I studied at Pitt. James also taught classes at Pitt and would invite me to be a guest speaker for his class relating to topics like co-occurring disorders and assessment and diagnostics in the behavioral health field. Thanks to the many kids at the Hillman Library who helped me with the computers and research so I could find needed information for my projects. All of you have made a difference in my life and inspired me to help others.

Ways to Promote Change

I will discuss external and internal change in this chapter and the challenges that come with it. Let's begin with making external changes. A very common thing that is heard in the field of addiction is changing People, Places and Things. In many cases, it serves as a cop-out because many clients and others attempting to become clean and sober say this because it's an easy answer. I would ask them to take it to the next level and be specific. Tell me who they plan on ending relationships with. This makes it more difficult and more real because now the person must personalize it.

This person must have the courage to tell someone they have been using drugs or alcohol with for many years that the relationship has ended because they are trying to change their life. Things become more and more real when a place that you frequented regularly is no longer part of your life. Lastly, things that you have done for years, and the lifestyle you have lived also have to change. By the time all of this has been done, your life is a clean slate.

The fact is making these changes is scary and hard work. Even more difficult, is trying to establish new friends, new places to go and new things to do in order to change your lifestyle and give yourself a fair chance at having a new life. Change is a frightening thing and particularly for those of us in Pittsburgh, Pennsylvania. After all, we were still paying ten cents at a payphone for nearly a decade while the rest of the country was paying a quarter. On a more personal note, I was using 8-track tapes while my friends and the rest of the world had cassette tapes. By the time I was using a cassette player, my friends and the rest of the world were pros with CDs and DVDs.

For those with addictions, this is particularly difficult because when you get rid of those in your life who use drugs or alcohol, there is no one left. I used to ask, in my own sarcastic way, how was I supposed to get a "sober support network" as many in my profession say? Do I go out on the street with a piece of cardboard around my neck that says, "I need a new sober support network, please call, 412-000-0000, if you are clean and sober and want to be my friend?"

I would ask friends to stop coming by my apartment with booze and weed, if they were under the influence or if they were locked out and needed a flop house because they were high and drunk, and their parents had locked them out. I made it clear that they meant a lot to me and that I would be more than happy to watch a game with them or get something to eat, but I was not interested in getting high anymore. What do you think the response was from my friends of 25 years and longer? They stopped coming to my apartment or having anything to do with me, and I was devastated because of it.

After about a month or two of licking my wounds and feeling betrayed, I realized that it was a blessing in disguise. Now I could study in the evening when I got home from my college classes. I no longer had people stopping by my house and kicking the door to knock because their hands were full with a case of beer and a fifth of liquor rolling

170

freely on top of the case, while they performed a balancing act to prevent the bottle from crashing to the ground.

To change places, I often stayed home and isolated myself because I still could not trust myself to be able to go to a bar where my "friends" were and not drink. I, like many of us, went through a phase where I would test myself to see if I could resist the temptation. I would go into the bar and order pop (aka, soda to the rest of the world). I would sit and socialize with my friends for an hour or so and turn down offers for a beer or answer questions about why I was drinking pop and no booze. I did this successfully a couple of times, and this led me to believe that I could go in and drink one beer for about thirty minutes while socializing with my "friends." Well, before long, I was drinking like a fish and consuming inordinate amounts of alcohol again.

To change things and to change my lifestyle, I became enveloped in my studies at school. College was my savior in changing all external factors. The fact is, college became my new drug of choice, and just as I drank to extreme, I studied to extreme. The more time I spent on campus, the less time I had to drink. My addictive personality took over and before long I realized how much I loved learning. I was spending 40-60 hours a week at school and even more during finals.

The people I was surrounded with were other students who were trying to better their life and position themselves in society to have a life of quality and financial security. I made new friends as we studied together and worked on projects and assignments together. And yes, occasionally we would go for drinks together but that was becoming less and less important. Reaching my goals in college and in life were becoming more and more important and my priority. I was finding out, slowly but surely, that there was more to life than getting drunk, arguing, fighting and getting arrested. As these things began to happen, internal changes were easier to make and to see.

In retrospect, internal changes were taking place that made making external changes possible as well. They work hand-in-hand. Telling myself and then believing that achievement of some of these goals were even possible (internal change) motivated me to do the work and make the changes needed to achieve external change, like studying on campus and at home and changing my lifestyle as discussed earlier.

I would like to show you the interventions and techniques that I have developed over the years that have worked for me personally and have worked for many of my clients. Let me be clear, that some of the interventions and techniques may or may not have been used in clinical or research trials.

What's important is that I have found them to be helpful for me in my personal recovery and in my professional experiences with clients. Keep in mind that in your journey to promote positive change, what works for one person may not work for another. This is true even with interventions and techniques that have been researched, and that is why the term, probability, is used in research. There can be an increase in the probability of it working but few, if any, are definitive or guaranteed to work.

Tricks of the Trade

Interventions and Techniques that have
worked for me and many of my clients.

In behavioral health (mental illness and addiction), there are different kinds of therapy and many different approaches, interventions and techniques to address different behaviors and diagnoses. I will share a few with you that I have found to be helpful for me and for clients I have worked with over the years.

Shared, will be practical approaches that I call *Do the Math* and a *Formula for Recovery and One for Relapse*. There are techniques to help with those that *procrastinate* and ways to *motivate* and not become *complacent*. Lastly, there are examples of the *cognitive process* to give a different and healthier perspective *and attitude*.

Do the Math

It is so easy to get caught up in our illness (anxiety, depression, addiction) or bad habits and behaviors (overeating and spending) and a variety of other things without even considering what we are really doing or the extent to which we are doing it.

When working with those with Substance Use Disorders (SUD) and Gambling, looking at the financial aspect of things can be a great awakening. It can be achieved by simply doing the math and calculating the amount of money that is being spent on your habit or disorder.

Ask your client or yourself how much is spent on each drug every week and then multiply it by fifty-two. You will be astounded at the amount of money used to pay for the drug dealers' Mercedes, while slowly ruining your life, your health and your financial future.

While working with a patient diagnosed with severe depression, he stated that he was depressed because of his financial situation. He was without heat during the cold Pittsburgh winter. His apartment was lit and heated with kerosene lamps. He said that he was at risk of being evicted. First and most importantly, I helped him get connected with the Low-Income Home Energy Assistance Program (LIHEAP).

The client said that this was the main reason that he was depressed, and that he had not had severe depression like this before, so I knew that it was primarily situational depression. I asked him how he was coping with the depression and he said, "I'm drinking because that is the only way I know how to deal with it." I knew that his depression was also caused by consuming alcohol, which is a depressant. The encouraging thing is that both can be treated and changed.

I asked him how much he was spending on his drinking and he estimated $30 a day. I know that many people who drink alcohol also smoke cigarettes, so I asked him how much he smoked, and he said, "Two packs a day." At that time cigarettes were $6 a pack. I asked about coffee consumption, because he worked in construction. I know that many construction workers stop at gas stations, stores and other outlets to buy cigarettes and coffee before they go to work. He told me about two cups a day with cups being about $2 a piece.

Let's do the math:

Thirty dollars a day for alcohol multiplied by 30 days is $900 every month.

Twelve dollars a day for cigarettes times thirty days is $360 a
   month and

Four dollars a day for coffee times 30 days is $120 every month.

I explained to him that he was spending $900 month on alcohol,
$360 a month on cigarettes and another $120 a month on coffee for
a total of $1,380 a month on those three products alone. I went on to
explain that if he cut this in half, he would have a lot more money.
I explained that if he just stopped the two big items, (cigarettes and
alcohol) he would have $1,260 a month, and if he just stopped drinking,
he would have $900 more a month. His rent was about $600 a month at
that time.

The difference of $300 could go toward his gas and electricity bills.
He could entirely change his situation and subsequently, his depression.
The look of amazement on his face after doing the math was worth
a million. He did not have a clue that he was spending that kind of
money, and that he had the power to change it, if he chose to do the
work necessary to change.

This example focuses primarily on the financial aspect and does not
include the damage alcohol and cigarettes do to a person's organs only to
cause severe health problems with asthma, COPD, emphysema and liver
problems like cirrhosis, while both affect the heart and the brain. This
creates an unhealthy cycle. The medical problems can affect personal
finances by missing work, paying more for life or health insurance,
hospital bills and prescribed medications.

It has become more and more common in my field for the chronic
opioid-addicted client to use ten to twenty bags of heroin a day. I have
heard clients claim they use as many as fifty bags of heroin daily. I can't
imagine how this is even possible without resulting in death, but this is
what I am told. Even if you use ten bags for $100 a day consumption,
you would add two zeros to 365 days in the year for a total value of
$36,500.00 a year for heroin use.

Strangely enough, most of these clients are unemployed and/or on a
fixed income which would only amount to an income under or around
$10,000 a year. Where is the other $26,500 coming from? This is not
to mention their rent, car payments, utilities, car insurance, bus fare,

groceries, child support (in some cases), cigarettes, coffee and much more.

Where do the other thousands of dollars come from? This is the reason for an increase in crime. To support their habit and pay for the many other things mentioned, people must borrow (and not pay back) or sell drugs. There are also a lot of retail theft, burglary and robbery crimes being committed. What is stolen is then sold for a fraction of its value, so the culprit can buy drugs to prevent going through withdrawal symptoms.

Working "under the table" is common as well. After all, those with addictions want the money now (immediate gratification) and will not be able to save for a pension or rainy day. If social security is still around when they retire, they will not get anything because they paid nothing into it. I use this same concept with clients as it relates to their treatment and recovery. In other words, if you do not invest anything in your recovery, you will not get anything back.

The clients, I currently work with, are required to have 2.5 hours of counseling every month which I find amazing because I expected that the requirements would be much more than that. So, let's do the math. Clients come to my office and tell me, "I only owe you a half hour because I already saw you for two hours of counseling this month." I ask them how many hours a day they spend being dope sick (having withdrawal symptoms), planning or scheming on how they are going to get the money for the drugs, the amount of time spent trying to sell something they own or have stolen. What is the amount of time they made phone calls, and then waited for the dope man to show up? What about the amount of time spent cooking up drugs, shooting it, and then the amount of time they spend high?

"From the time I got up until the time I went to sleep or passed out is a common answer." The answer is at least eight to as many as sixteen hours a day. I then ask them to give me a little more than eight hours a day times thirty days in the month. To be exact, eight hours and twenty minutes a day would equal 250 hours a month is invested in their addiction.

I then tell them, let's do the math. The 2.5 hours regulation for counseling is 1% of the 250 hours he/she spends destroying their mind, body and spirit for many years, as opposed to the one percent of that same time, to help them turn their entire life around.

The last example I will share is: ***Abstinence*** + ***Change*** = ***Recovery***.

Without change, there is just abstinence. A person that is abstinent but has not changed their thinking, the people they associate with, the places they go and the things that they do is **Dry** not **Clean**. This is where the term "Dry Drunk" comes from.

Someone that is dry and not clean is usually miserable because nothing else has changed. In fact, they are likely to be unhappy and discontent. I remember going to the bar to hang with friends and having soda while the others there were drinking. I hung on for one or two times. It was like holding on for dear life, with my dead body weight making every moment more and more difficult to hold on. The greatest relief came when I finally gave in and fell, so to speak. After the tenth time I was offered a drink by my buddies I said, okay, give me a shot and a beer.

Over the years, I have developed my own formula that I have seen play out more times than I can count and that is:

Vulnerability + ***Access*** = ***Relapse*** (or simply using drugs again) if a period of abstinence has not been established.

If someone is not doing well and having a lot of problems, is depressed, lost a job, has recently gotten divorced, filed bankruptcy or a million other things that can make us vulnerable, we are more likely to use drugs or alcohol if they are accessible. If drugs or alcohol are not accessible, we would have to work to get them.

This is similar in the field of mental health if/when someone is suicidal. When I worked as a care manager, I took triage calls all hours of the night from clients that were in crisis and contemplating suicide. One of the most important things a clinician needs to know is if he or she has access to a weapon. If the answer was yes, we then would ask them to give the weapon/s to a friend or family member and let them hold those weapons until further notice.

Many say or think that if a person really wants to use the drug they will. If a person really wants to kill themselves, they will. Ultimately this is true. However, if not immediately accessible, the person needs to work to get that drug or weapon and could change their mind in the time it would take them to get the drug or the weapon.

By the time I stopped drinking there were limited places I could go to drink because I had been thrown out of so many of them, including the one right around the corner from my apartment. This became a blessing in disguise because I was frequently vulnerable and wanted to go get drunk. To do that, I had to get a bus or walk a long way to get to a bar I could drink at. On a cold winter night, pouring rain, and other circumstances, I would decide to stay in my apartment, not drink and just be miserable. I saved a lot of money and potential liver damage over the years by not having access.

On the other hand, if there is access because a friend stops over with a cold case of beer and some weed, and you are strong and doing well, most likely, you will be able to assert yourself and turn him or her away.

There are a lot of doctors and nurses that are addicted to drugs these days. They are first responders and see death, injury and are around sick people all the time. In addition, they work long hours and long shifts and cannot escape. Nurses and doctors have great responsibility and people's lives are literally in their hands, making them two of the more vulnerable professions. Nurses and doctors are two positions where they have easy access to drugs whether they are pills, fentanyl patches or injectables.

This doesn't mean that you can never spend time with those that drink or use drugs. However, I don't think it is healthy for anyone to be around people who are using a substance that controlled their life on a regular basis. If I were to start going to bars and cafés regularly, I would have to ask why I am choosing to frequent places that make me vulnerable and give me immediate access.

Bottom line, if you are in a bad mood or state of mind, if things aren't going well for you and you are miserable for whatever reason, stay away from drugs and alcohol. If you are in a good place in life, don't overestimate and be around drugs and alcohol any more than you must.

I remember the Rodney Dangerfield line, "No respect, no respect!" I have chosen to give the ultimate respect to drugs and alcohol because I know that they had power over me and over my life for many years. I give drugs and alcohol enough respect to say that those chemical substances are more powerful than I am and for that reason, I will not touch them again unless I am willing to take the chance of losing control again.

I stress that when we become clean and sober, it is crucial to be humble or you will be humbled by the same drugs and alcohol that brought you down in the first place. Take the high road.

Putting Things in Perspective

It is easy to lose perspective, when all you have been focused on for years were drugs, alcohol, arguing, fighting and trying to avoid and escape anything and everything. When a person thinks negatively all the time, then everything becomes negative, even if/when it isn't. Perspective is limited or even lost when decisions are based on feelings. For example, if something feels good, it doesn't mean that it is good for you. Drugs make you feel good, but while you're feeling good your world is in the process of falling apart. More is better right? Just kidding. However, more is better to the addict until it kills them.

On the contrary, because something hurts doesn't mean that it is not good for you. Think about having a hip or knee replacement surgery as an example. For the person to have long lasting relief and be free from the excruciating pain, the pain of being cut open, and the painful physical rehabilitation needs to happen in order to heal, strengthen that area, and have long-term relief.

Another example is weightlifting. For those who have never lifted or have gone a long time without and allowed themselves to get out of shape as I have, doing bicep curls the first couple of times is extremely painful. But, in order to become strong and fit, the weightlifter must work through the pain to reap the benefits. If you ask the weightlifter if it was worth the hard work, more than likely they will tell you it was.

I have learned to put my negative experiences to work for me. I have been very open and honest with the information shared and will not stop now. I still fall into traps where I get caught up in the injustices to me and begin to feel sorry for myself. When I decide that it is time to pull myself out of the ditch I was choosing to sit in, here are some things that I have learned to do:

1) **I look back on the hell I was once living in**, then I look at what I am feeling sorry for myself about and all of a sudden, it looks like no big deal. I look at the countless wonderful things I now have in my life and then begin to feel foolish for whining about such a minute thing in comparison to where I once was. Sometimes, I have literally slapped myself in the face and told myself to wake up and remember that my life is better than I ever expected it to be. Then, I look at how so many others are struggling with this thing called life. This process helps me to transition from a mindset of bitterness, frustration and sometimes depression and anger, to being thankful and grateful which is a complete turnaround in a brief period.

2) *__Imagery__* is another technique that I use specifically for relapse prevention purposes. I have known many people who have relapsed after a significant period of sobriety. I believe that this is often because people don't know that the severity of their problems while they were using drugs inevitably faded over time.

A friend I have known since we were four years old had fought through his addiction to achieve many years of sobriety. Within one year, he had lost all that he had gained in those many years and then ultimately, his own life. I try to keep fresh in my mind the nightmare I lived every day when I was drinking.

I sit quietly in a dark room and review every detail possible during my life as a drunk. I remember waking up in the morning with my sheets drenched with sweat. I remember my head throbbing with pain with every beat of my heart. I remember feeling hot but freezing cold at the same time.

I get out of bed and go to the bathroom and look in the mirror. My face looks as red as a ripe tomato, and my hair is going in five different directions. I have to rinse my mouth out so I can swallow and drink cold water due to dry pipes, as we used to call it.

I step into a scalding hot shower and feel like I am going to either suffocate from the heat or sweat to death. While washing my hair, I can feel pain as I run my hands over the lump on my head and the burning from the still open cuts on my face and body from old and new injuries. I get out of the shower and feel somewhat human.

I begin to feel the tremors, and literally, shake like a leaf. I forget about the lumps and open cuts and run the comb right through them and outwardly yell "Ahhhhh!" followed by some profanity. I also realize that my ears are ringing because of the intense hangover. I know that this and the tremors are not going to stop until I get a few belts of booze in me.

I get out of the shower and smell the smoke that is caked in the sweatshirt and jeans I wore the night before and imagine what my lungs are enduring after breathing in secondary smoke for several hours, in addition to, the pack or two I smoked last night. I cough up some yellow stuff and feel a burning in my chest.

After getting dressed, I step outside and must use both hands to block the glaring sun. It takes about two or three minutes before my eyes can adjust. I hustle to get some booze to take the edge off, and then it is time to party. I go to a party and remember knowing a ton of people at the party but still feeling alone. I begin guzzling, whether it is beer or alcohol. I drink inordinate amounts in a short period of time. Then it's time to stagger home as I've done several times a week.

I remember the hopeless feeling when I begin to lose my balance. I know that I am going to hit that sidewalk hard and know that there isn't a damn thing I can do about it. I fall several times on my way home. I get up on both feet and look up and as soon as I stand up, my momentum takes me forward, and I pick up speed for several steps and then I'm down again.

I look at the nearest telephone pole or tree and that is my target to grab onto. What would take me fifteen minutes or so when I am not obliterated, will take me an hour or more to walk home. When I get to the back door of my basement apartment, I will take another ten to fifteen minutes to find the keyhole and unlock the door.

I learned to save time by closing one eye in order to accurately put the key in the hole. I will forget about the pipe that must have been measured for my forehead and walk right into it. I will scream obscenities at the top of my lungs at 3 AM in the morning.

I use my left shoulder to slide along the wall of the building until I make it to my apartment door. It will take me another several minutes to slide my right hand along the wall until I am able to find and lift the light switch in the hallway. I will unlock the door, take my clothes off and pass out.

Following this exercise, I open my eyes look around at my house and my reasonably new car parked in front of the house. I go to the dining room window and look out to see our big backyard with the clean lines in the grass that was just cut. I look at and hug my precious wife. I locate our three handsome pets and show them some love. Then I ask myself, do I want the old life that I just briefly revisited or do I want to keep the life I have today? I assure you that there is no contest.

When using imagery, it is important to try and get in touch with all five senses. I concentrate to the point that I can feel the pain from the sweat getting into my brush-burned knees from falling on my walk home from the party, smelling the smoke in my clothes and my dirty socks and on and on. In doing that, you are coming as close to reliving it as possible.

The technique of imagery helps me to relive these bad experiences but in a controlled way because I am taking myself back to that moment when I staggered and fell or back to the moment I woke up and felt the burning of my knees as opposed to the car backfiring when least expected. The former was causing a sudden jolt of upset, the latter is a controlled re-creation of the experience. By doing this, I assure myself that I will never forget how bad things really were, and I will be less likely to minimize the potential consequences of relapsing.

I have had many patients that have relapsed tell me that, "I wanted to reward myself after being clean for that long." If I am remembering how bad it really was by reliving it through this imagery exercise, I will be less likely to ever think that by returning to drugs or alcohol is rewarding in any way.

3) ***Look at the amount of time that you invested in destroying your life*** because it could help put in perspective that you need time to turn things around. When I drank and smoked marijuana, I got the result (euphoria) I wanted in minutes or

even seconds. This explains why getting high is referred to as immediate gratification.

For twenty-four years, every day that I got high (which was almost every day), I got the results I was looking for every day. This made it very difficult for me to accept that it would take a long time to turn my dark and self-destructed world around. I couldn't just sit, roll a joint and guzzle a couple of beers and have my whole life change to the way I would like. My late and eternally wise mother told me one day that, "If you put even a fraction of time and effort into your school work as the time and effort you put into getting money and drink, there is no stopping you."

4) ***See yourself completing a task or goal successfully*** – This is another example of imagery, in that you are imagining that you are completing a task or a goal successfully. Many might think, "How is thinking about something going to make it happen?" Well, you are right to some degree in that, you can't just sit there and smoke crack and play on your PlayStation 16 hours a day and sleep the other eight and expect to get the job you just saw yourself getting in your head.

Stay with me though. You can go to a job interview worrying about how you are going to present yourself. What happens is, you start stuttering and your worry shines right through. You will present as an insecure scared person who is lacking confidence. Then you get to say that you are right and continue to be unemployed.

On the other hand, you see yourself going into the job interview as a confident person, answering questions articulately and with confidence. You are more likely to be hired than the person who was worried and did not see themselves getting the job. Of the two candidates, who would you hire? To reiterate, that doesn't mean that you would get the job, but your chances of getting it would be much better.

Acronyms

Acronyms are something that I have always liked because they are short and sweet and make important messages easy to remember. I need that and so, too, do my clients. I will begin with my favorite, HALT. HALT stands for Hungry, Angry, Lonely, and Tired. It is said in the recovery community that when you endorse all four of these it means you need a meeting or help and support. It doesn't matter whether the problem involves Depression, Schizophrenia, Bipolar Disorder or Substance Use Disorders (SUD) like alcoholism and drug addiction.

I had endorsed all four of the HALT elements almost constantly (or so it seemed), for many years. Most people use the H in HALT as literally hungry and without food, but I think that the H could mean many different things because people can be hungry for many different things. This is because I was never without food. My mom had to ration food and buy cheap food that wasn't always the healthiest for us, but I was never really starving for food and unfortunately, there are those that are.

H--For many years I was Hungry for love and for someone to care about me. I was hungry for happiness which I had little of. I was Hungry for independence that I was incapable of due to my variety of disabilities. I was Hungry to find a reason to live and to find myself. I was an empty shell that was living in the darkness, depression, hopelessness and helplessness of the world.

A--The first thing I felt when I got up in the morning was Angry. Angry simply because I woke up and would have to live another day. I would have to do this without all the things that I was hungry for. My day frequently involved an internal fight because I was ambivalent about taking my life. I asked myself if I should kill myself or keep getting as drunk as I could to get through another day. My anger often led to verbal and physical fights because of the life I was living at home and in the streets.

What I have learned about anger is that it is evoked by something happening different from the way you would like. You also get mad because you care. Think about it! If you get mad because someone says something ignorant to you, the anger is because you can't stop them

183

from saying it. Because of that, we beat them up not only for what they said, but also to make sure that the beating will stop them from saying it again, unless they are plain stupid and like getting beaten.

If you don't care what is said to you, you are less likely to get angry about it. It's probably still the same today, but when I was growing up, if you wanted to get someone mad, you said something about their mother, and then the fight was on. Well, many years after I got control of my anger and became sober, I got in an argument with someone and of course, he had to say that my mother was a whore. In my drinking days, we would have been fighting. Instead, I told him that I heard she charged a high price and asked if he got his money's worth. He was stunned by my response, and the look on his face was worth a million. I walked away with a smile on my face instead of a bloody nose with him being taken off to the hospital and me going to jail.

When I lived in anger, it took so much of me, it made me unlikeable. I was unpredictable, especially when I was drinking. At times, I was referred to as Dr. Jekel and Mr. Hyde. People would say that I was the nicest guy in the world when I was sober but didn't want to be near me when I was drinking.

This is a nice segue for the next letter in HALT and that is lonely.

L--Lonely was another one that really got to me. I experienced it every day, almost all day. Even the friends that I was with every day, I often questioned if they really cared about me and really liked me. I have always had a problem with this. I guess one reason is because of the kids that liked me in school, and then it all changed when they saw me having a seizure. They would act like they didn't know me after that.

Then there is the internal loneliness that I carried with me all the time, regardless of the circumstances. Most of this is because I didn't like myself and who I was. I would go to parties and know almost everyone and still feel alone.

Loneliness is also a state of mind because you can be around many and feel alone. On the other hand, you can be alone and not be lonely. I have a friend that lost her husband to drugs, and though I'm sure she has her moments, she has learned to be okay with being alone. She tells me that it is because she is not alone because she has God. She says that this has given her a sense of peace because unlike human beings, He is always there and can be depended on.

I can relate to this because since I have become closer to God and to my faith, I too am more at peace, whether I am with someone or not. One might think that this is easy for me to say now that I am married, and this might be true to a degree. However, loneliness began to decrease long before I met my wife. This is because I reintroduced myself to the God I was introduced to when I was a child. I had faded from him over the years. By no means am I trying to convert anyone. I'm simply giving another way that my friend and I have made ourselves feel fulfilled and complete when we might otherwise feel lonely.

I remember a time when I hated being alone. A wise man told me that I hate being alone because when I am, I hate the company that I am alone with. I have never forgotten that. It proved to be true because today, I like to spend time alone and regroup, relax and take time for myself. This is because I like who I am and who I have become since my days of loneliness.

T--Tired is the last one of the four. There is a healthy tired and an unhealthy tired. This T is of course referring to the unhealthy tired. This is when you can get no rest. I remember the depression keeping me in bed for days because what was going on mentally made an impact on me physically. I was always exhausted because of the battle that was going on in my head every day. It was a challenge just to get out of bed.

I had to fight to live another day, to find the booze and weed to get me through that day. I had to fight the seizures, my poor self-esteem and lack of self-confidence. I had to fight verbally and physically with people. I was fighting the racing thoughts, anxiety and all the other symptoms that come with all my different mental health issues and withdrawal symptoms from all the drugs and alcohol I was using.

All this fighting, with very few breaks, results in physical, emotional and spiritual exhaustion and tiredness. I wanted to just throw in the towel and quit, but something kept waking me up every day. Endorsing one of the four letters from HALT can be a challenge but living with all four of them most of the time is brutal.

To prevent ever going back to this lonely state, when I become stressed out, I check to see if I am Hungry, Angry, Lonely or Tired.

Whether it is one, two, three or all four that I am endorsing, I try to do whatever it takes to resolve or erase them so that I can be back on course. I can schedule an appointment with my therapist, my minister or some other person from my parish. I can try calling a friend, taking a nap, going to the gym for a massage or a trip to the steam room.

I love listening to music and soft jazz when times get tougher than usual. I like taking rides in the country, unless angry is one of the four. Being behind the wheel of a car, may not be a great idea when angry. Whether it be the first or last option, praying to God for strength is always a good idea.

The challenge/s I am faced with, and the timing of them, helps to determine how I am going to deal with it. If the option I choose is not as effective as I would like, I will try something new until I find something that works to relieve any or all of the HALT elements. This is how I have developed a repertoire to battle different symptoms and problems over the years.

The Two Es

The two Es stand for Explanation versus Excuse. This is primarily used with the clients I work with but can be helpful for me or anyone else. It is common for just about anyone, but particularly those with criminal records, addictions and/or mental health problems. These three populations are prone to making excuses and not taking responsibility for their behaviors. I can say this because I have a mental health diagnosis, I have a criminal record, and I have an addiction. Clients have admittedly done this on numerous occasions.

Earlier in my career, I worked with convicted sex offenders. Approximately half or more of them had been sexually abused, and this was often their excuse for committing the crime for which they were convicted. Adults that abuse their kids or significant other say that they became an abuser because they were abused when they were a kid.

I explain to the client that the first step toward change is taking responsibility for their behavior. When saying that they are an abuser because they were abused, what they are really saying is because I was abused, I can't help myself or control myself and therefore, I am not responsible.

I ask them to imagine telling this to a judge in court. I think it is a safe guess that the judge would not say, "Okay that explains it. Not guilty because the abuser was abused." On the contrary, the judge is more likely to say something like, "That is exactly why I think that you should be incarcerated."

Think about this! By saying that you are an abuser because you were abused, you are also saying that you will always be an abuser because you will always be someone that was abused. This person is saying that they cannot and will not ever change.

Violence was a frequent occurrence in the home we grew up in, and I was often on the receiving end of it, whether it was from either of my brothers, my father or my grandmother. This explains a lot about why I became violent, but by no means did it excuse my violent behavior. I know, personally, that it would not be excused because I became labeled an incorrigible child (as they called us back then). Subsequently, I became part of the juvenile justice system where I was incarcerated several times for seven years of my life as a minor. I was incarcerated as an adult more than once as well, which is proof that the judge will hold a person responsible for an illegal behavior despite being an abused child.

Stealing from someone cannot be excused or justified because you were stolen from. Being poor might be the explanation for someone caught stealing food for his family, but it is still theft. It is an illegal act, and it is wrong. It is easy to understand why they did that, but it is still illegal.

For long-term change to occur, I had to man-up and take responsibility for my own behavior. Whether the violence was because I was abused, I was angry, someone offended me, and I was drunk or just having a bad day, it could not be excused. I knew I had to change, and that it would take hard work. In fact, I still struggle with built up and built in resentment, hostility and anger.

I cannot be using things that happened to me years ago as an excuse for my current behavior. I am pushing sixty years of age and blaming my behavior/s on things that happened forty to more than fifty years ago is irrational.

It is very common for an offender to become a victim when they are confronted and being held responsible for their behavior. Watch the show, COPS, and you will see people that have become pros at playing the victim when caught. It's sad but amusing when I watch that show because no matter what the situation, the crime, a male or a woman, there is a certain process that takes place. Watch closely to see how things evolve.

There will be a person of authority (the police) confronting them about what they allegedly did. This could be a crime that was reported, a bad plate or sticker on the car, a fight, anything. There is manipulation, lying, deceit, conning, explaining things away and making excuses. When the cops conclude that the person is to be arrested, the person becomes aggressive and fights them. When the police get control, they become submissive and say something like, "Okay officer, I'm sorry, I give up, I give up."

Then it is time for them to talk about all the things that the police did wrong in handling the situation, and that their rights have been violated and they are suing. They want the police officers' badge numbers so they can report them. Almost always, before they are taken to jail, they beg (in a whining tone) to smoke a cigarette.

I remember during my partying days, when people I knew that sold drugs and others that stole things thinking that they were smooth when they were getting away with it. Those same people would turn infantile when they got busted and begin to cry. I must admit that I was a crier too a couple of times. Alcohol can break down all the walls and make tough guys cry. I saw guys tougher than I, fall to tears.

The bottom line is that all of us are responsible for our own behavior regardless of what we have endured and survived. Our current problems or behaviors can be explained by what we have been through, but it does not excuse the behavior for which there will be consequences at some point. I frequently convey this to my patients and try to remember this for my own good.

<u>The 2 Ps</u>

The 2 Ps are *Protect* and *Provide* and are directed toward patients I work with who are parents. It has become far too common for parents to be at risk of losing custody of their children due to their behaviors defined as abusive. Abuse can occur in two primary forms and they are: 1) The Commission of abuse and 2) The Omission of abuse.

The commission of abuse relates to an act that causes mental, physical, verbal or sexual abuse. Beating the child excessively, calling them names and treating them in a demeaning way and child molestation are just a few examples. On the other hand, omission of abuse relates to what the parent fails to do for their child, otherwise known as child neglect. Examples of child neglect are not feeding them, leaving them home alone, without food, without clothing suitable for weather conditions, leaving them in the car on a hot summer day, while the parent goes into the bar to drink.

We are quick to hear people say, "That's against my rights." In counseling sessions, I stress to clients that being a parent is a privilege not a right, and that it is the right of the child to be protected and provided for because they are too young to do that for themselves. For this reason, the parent/s has/have custody of their child and if they do not protect and provide, the state of Pennsylvania will. Ironically, your parental rights can be revoked. To clarify, no one has a right to be a parent, but once they become a parent, they have parental rights that can be taken from them.

My wife and I were foster parents for a brief period, and many different things were required before we became foster parents. We had to complete forty to fifty hours of parenting training. Our finances had to be stable, which means that we had to open all our personal information to strangers. We had to show proof of salary. Both of us had to have respectable credit scores and proof that we paid our bills on time and more.

I recall a person in our parenting training class becoming offended when they said that all potential foster parents had to submit their bank records, credit scores and salaries. He thought that they were intruding on his privacy. I did not feel offended or violated because I completely understood why this was required. My wife and I had no problem doing what was asked because we understood that they do not want to take these kids from one unfortunate situation and place them in another.

To further my point, I tell clients that prior to becoming a parent, if they want to go out all night, getting high and God knows what else, they would be harming themselves. However, when they become a parent that all changes, because they now have an obligation as parents to take care of their children. This means doing what it takes to get themselves as healthy as possible. This includes abstaining from drugs and alcohol, being responsible and changing their lifestyle. Most importantly, it means that their child or children come first. This is a big shift because when addicted, the focus is on themselves.

Once you become a parent, there are parental rights, but until then, it is a privilege to be a parent because there are many that would love to be parents and can't, whether it be because of a medical problem, age, disability or some other reason.

My wife and I were foster parents for a brief period, and it was a great experience and a privilege. We were amazed at the loops we had to jump through to earn that privilege but completely understood. What I struggle to understand is how we, as older adults, who had good credit, owned a home and had good jobs needed this training, but people who are unemployed, very young and immature (some minors) can be parents with no training required just because they give birth to a baby. Many of these children will end up in the foster-care system and will not get the care that they need and deserve. This perpetuates the problem because it is common that many in foster care are there because their parents cannot provide due to being in the criminal justice system, are addicted to drugs, and in fact, die from the lifestyle they are living. Many of these foster children end up becoming parents who are addicted to drugs, go to jail and have their children taken from them.

It's not even headline news anymore to hear that a child was taken by authorities due to the parents having their kids live in deplorable conditions. They are absent parents because they are out getting high. They are negligent parents because they are on the streets committing crimes and doing drugs. This is not to say that all young parents do drugs and are incapable of being good parents though.

What I do know is that the above was the situation that many of my clients have put themselves and their kids in. They now must report to the county authorities, Children, Youth, and Families (CYF). The other common outcome to avoid foster care is that these poor grandparents that have already raised their own kids now have to take care of these young and energetic children until they are eighteen or until the parents get them back. This is if they have not overdosed and died, and if they meet the requirements to get the children back.

My wife and I fostered two children who had the same mother and different fathers. Mom was smoking crack cocaine, and one of the two fathers was incarcerated when we had them. We showed up at Family Court and their mother was still smoking crack cocaine and was pregnant with another child that would be delivered shaking erratically as I had when seizing. This child would begin life this way, by no choice of its own. They could have birth defects, learning disabilities, brain damage and more. This sad situation was avoidable, had this woman stopped using drugs and/or chosen to use protection until she was healthy and could protect and provide for her children.

The 2 Ps have been an eye opener for some of my clients that are open to changing. They do want to have their kids back and are beginning to understand that there is a life outside of drugs. I often get that "Never thought of it that way" look.

Over the many years I have been sober, I have learned to apply things like the two Ps to my life, even if it does not fit with the specific details originally intended. For example, I don't have children, so you may not think that the two Ps apply. But I tell myself that it is a Privilege to have my wonderful wife and my three special pets, and I have a duty to Protect and Provide for them. I use this thought to motivate myself to remain clean and sober and keep doing the right thing. This keeps me grounded, humble and rich with information and examples of how I can remain healthy and not be a hypocrite.

Ways to Motivate

The famous, Booker T. Washington said, "Idle hands are the devil's workshop". The inference I get from this famous quote is that, if I sit

191

around and do nothing, I am more likely to get into something that is not so good.

In my drinking days, I was asked more times than I could count if I had any plans or goals for my life. The simple answer was "Yeah". I want to get as much booze today and get as drunk as possible. In other words, no. I had no goals or plans. Bottom line is that you can't work toward something when you don't know what it is that you want. That is the biggest barrier to being motivated. Priorities are motivators. It's just that sometimes, what we prioritize, and the goals generated from those priorities, can be very irrational and unhealthy.

For example, addiction gets so bad and so intense that the addict prioritizes that chemical substance over their children, their house, their freedom, their job and ultimately, their life. Because drugs and alcohol have hit my own family, I know firsthand that those addicted to drugs don't get out of bed until 11 am or 12 pm and their partying lasts well into the early morning hours (3 am – 5 am). However, treatment of addiction at a methadone clinic reflects something far different.

We open for business at 6 am and have 30-60 people and sometimes more, standing in line waiting for the gate to open. This means that the majority of our patients got out of bed at 4 am - 4:30 am, so that they could commute by bus and get to our program by 5:30 am – 6 am to drink methadone before they return home or go to work. When I began working at a methadone clinic, I was astounded then and still now, by the number of people in line at that hour to get their methadone.

I can almost guarantee that if these same clients were told that if they had to get up at this ungodly hour and take a bus and get there by 5:30 am- 6 am, and they would be given a free bag of groceries, the answer would be something like, "Are you crazy?" "No way!" I know this because I have asked my clients if they would do this for a bag of free food and received a similar answer to the one above, coupled with a guilty grin or smile.

This is clear evidence that most of the people that I work with will get out of bed at a ridiculous hour to get their dose of methadone before they would do the same for a free bag of groceries for their kids. This shows how important methadone is to our clients, and how powerful of a motivator it is. This is also why our clients are not allowed to get their medication and leave the clinic, until they complete their counseling session. It's unfortunate that their medication is used as leverage to get them to stay for counseling. This is not the case with all, but many.

Let's focus on something that we are all guilty of at one time or another and that is ***procrastination.*** It is so important that we don't couple motivation with feeling. Though procrastination relates to everyone, it is particularly difficult for me and the addicted population for which I work. This is because we often view things based on how it makes you feel, (if it feels good, do it), (if it doesn't feel good, don't do it). If I waited until I felt like it or felt good about cleaning the house, it would never get cleaned.

Procrastinating is something we all are guilty of, and it is a barrier to progress, change and self-improvement. I have a sign hanging in my office that says, "Life is no remote, get up and change it yourself." There is another expression, "Idle hands are the devil's workshop". This applies to everyone but particularly those who are addicted and have mental health problems, because we are experts at not getting things done.

Prior to the big changes that occurred in my life, I procrastinated all the time. We are also experts at making excuses and getting ourselves to believe things we know are not true. We are experts at using defense mechanisms like, minimizing, denying, rationalizing, justifying, excusing, explaining away and distorting things in order to support what our goal is at that time. That goal is usually to not do anything because we don't feel like it or to do something that will only compound our problems.

For example, when you want to use drugs but know you shouldn't, you tell yourself, "I'll just do it this one time", knowing in the back of your mind that this one time will turn into two and three times, and you will be off to the races. One might believe this the first or second time they relapse, but the person that has relapsed many times before, knows that using just once is a lie. If you think about it, a person that smokes a pack of cigarettes a day quits nineteen times a day.

Minimizing would be saying that your problem can't be that bad because you still go to work every day. I had to use other stupid explanations because I did not work when I was in the pit of my addictions. You might be working, but I can guarantee your quality of work has suffered. Your relationship with coworkers isn't like it used to be. You are likely calling off and taking days off more than you did before you relapsed or lost control.

Even if this has not happened yet, it will, if drug and alcohol use doesn't stop. The one thing you will be doing is working to support your addiction. The money you work so hard for goes to the drug man or the bar owner. I include drug use because doing the wrong thing is also procrastinating in my opinion. It is a behavior that creates a barrier to getting things done.

I have learned about myself and my tactics, and this has helped me to catch myself in a lie and change it. I have also learned that things are much simpler when I catch myself and just go and do it, whatever it might be. I know if I keep putting it off, it will never get done, and things will not get better and will likely get worse, depending on what it is.

So much of procrastination has to do with lack of motivation or some other barrier to completing a specific task. Many ask me if you must be motivated to get the job done. For me the answer is yes and no. Not very helpful, right? For example, not many are excited or motivated to pick up dog poop, clean the basement, the dishes or many other things, but these things need to be done if you don't want the authorities to declare your house unsafe to live in or any other extreme reasons you can think of (disease, health department).

I know that I cannot do anything partially, so I have learned ways to trick myself into *doing* things instead of tricking myself to *not* do things. I tell myself to just clean a portion of a room knowing that it is not likely I will stop there, but it helps me to get started.

My wife and I split the household duties, and my job is to keep the living room and dining room clean on the first floor and her room is the kitchen. Like many American homes, if we don't watch out, the dining room table becomes the collection area for all the mail, magazines, laptop, books and much more. My priority, however, is the living room because that is where more of our time is spent watching TV, having company, writing my book and listening to music.

I know that I am sore, and my back is hurting and if I sit down, it will not get done. I start cleaning the dining room, and then it is finally done. After dusting, picking things up and vacuuming the floors, I am tired and sore, but the house is clean, and I feel good about what I have done and can see the difference.

I promise myself that I will, at least, vacuum the living room floor and pick up any clutter. What happens is that after I do these things, I tell myself that the room looks better. To really get it right though, I need to dust the furniture, clean the windows and any other glass in the room. When I complete this, I now have a genuinely clean room. Everything looks and smells fresh. The problem is that by cleaning the living room, the dining room now looks even worse than it had because the living room is pristine.

I begin to think that if I sit down, my back and neck pain will take over, and I will not be able to get up to do any more work. I get that last wind and do what is needed to match the pristine living room with a pristine dining room. By now, I am ready to collapse and rightfully so. I have just completed two major tasks with one to two hours of nearly non-stop work.

In reference to using alcohol, there were countless times when I told myself that I would have just one or two drinks before I almost drank the bar or liquor store dry. The difference is that instead of manipulating myself into doing something unhealthy for an alcoholic (drinking), I am manipulating myself into doing something to create a pleasant living environment.

The invisible benefits are the positive feelings of accomplishment and an improved mood by having a clean and uncluttered area. Making my wife happy isn't a bad thing, either. The pain from doing the work might be a negative, but the positives outweigh the negatives.

This may not sound like a big deal for the young men and women out there, but for an old man that has had all the accidents and injuries I have over the years, that is a lot of work. This is also why I usually do this on weekends. I know that I will need a day or two to recuperate so that I can go to work on Monday.

I know, in the back of my mind, that even though I had committed to just a portion of the living room, that most likely, I would complete the entire room, if not, the living room and dining room. The most important thing in completing tasks and getting things done is to get started. Procrastination is just another word for delay. To avoid delay, as the company Nike advises, just do it!

Complacency is another motivation killer. In fact, I encourage people to take time to enjoy and be proud of their accomplishments and rejuvenate themselves. However if we relax for too long and don't continue to set goals and raise the bar so to speak, the chances of returning to past behaviors increases. Booker T. Washington's famous expression is something that I think about when I start to get too comfortable.

There are two more examples that I have found helpful for me personally and have seemed to be enlightening for my clients. The first example is, you're asked to remember driving out in the country on a very hot and humid day when you come upon a small body of water. When you look, you see that it is covered with algae. How and why are all the algae able to develop? It is because of the lack of movement of the water for a certain length of time that has allowed this to happen.

Though this is extreme, when a person stays in bed for a long period with little movement or activity, the result is bedsores, loss of muscle mass and strength. As we get older, we are encouraged to do puzzles, read and other things to keep the mind active, to stay alert and be able to think clearly. Doctors have said that activity will slow the process of senility, dementia and Alzheimer's disease.

The second example relates to car accidents. As you have probably heard, a high percentage of accidents occur close to a person's home. Some say that the reason is that people became too relaxed and comfortable when they are in familiar territory. Subsequently, a person is less alert and less attentive to their surroundings.

I make a concerted effort to never become too comfortable for fear that I will drop my guard. Every day, from the time I get up until the time I go to bed, I try to stay in tune with my internal and external world. With the mental health problems and addiction problems that I have had, I am vulnerable to fall if I am not on top of my game.

Many have asked me how I can stay in tune to all these different things all the time because it sounds exhausting. I tell them that I am frequently exhausted anyhow, and don't know how much of it is for that reason. After all, I have PTSD and ADHD, so I have been anxious and uncomfortable as far back as I can remember. To me, it is well worth the effort to stay on top of things to prevent relapsing whether it be with alcohol or mental health problems.

To keep myself motivated and busy, I have decided to become part of the solution instead of part of the problem. For example, I am a recovering addict and work with the addicted population. I grew up in a home with domestic abuse and today, I am active with the FISA Foundation that tries to prevent domestic abuse and rape.

I have epilepsy that has been in remission for a long time but have stayed involved with the Epilepsy Foundation of Western Pennsylvania. I give money to help with research to find better treatments and a possible cure one day. I have presented about pertinent issues relating to this population, as well as, telling my story as someone that has lived with epilepsy and the struggles that come with it. I am a graduate of The University of Pittsburgh's School of Social Work and stay connected with the school in a variety of ways. I am a board member with the school's alumni association.

Please remember that reaching certain milestones and accomplishing goals does not mean that your work has ended. What it does mean is that you are now at a new level and can begin focusing on new tasks and goals to stay busy, active, productive and out of the devil's workshop, as Booker T. Washington called idle hands.

What Is a Real Tough Guy or Tough Person?

When people are hurting and struggling, it is often human nature to put on a happy face or even a tough guy face as a façade to hide or mask their fears, insecurities and anxiety. Though this can include anyone, it is particularly true with those that are vulnerable like the addicted and mental health populations. Though this is present in both genders, the male population finds it more important to hide their vulnerabilities.

There are exceptions and they are those with sociopathy, but most of these so-called tough guys are big teddy bears. Usually, they are men with a little boy inside of them that just want someone to love them. I remember a man that stood about six feet five inches and three hundred fifty pounds who was involved in gang activity. He was being seen for

Post-Traumatic Stress Disorder after a friend was shot and died in his arms.

This man, that was huge in stature, was a little boy whose family was the street because of the lack of family and nurturing in the home. His life had become one of anger, drugs, alcohol, weapons and violence. He was very guarded for quite a while and early on, made it clear that he didn't believe that he could benefit from counseling. He insisted that life is the way it is and was generally accepting that what happened to his friend would likely happen to him some day.

However, after working with me for a few months this tough guy dropped his guard and once he did, progress began and tears flowed. I came to find that this physically intimidating man's life had been a nightmare. I also came to find that he had feelings that he refused to show early on. Once he saw therapy as an opportunity to get the hurt and anger from years of violence out of him from one emotional wounding after another, he began to find hope.

When his time in therapy was about to end, I told him that though everyone thought that he was this huge sized tough guy, I knew that he was just a big teddy bear. He smiled, and said something like, "I am but you're the only one that knows this, and it is our secret." He smiled, and we shook hands at which time my white skinned hand was swallowed by and disappeared into his dark brown skinned hand. At the same time, he unexpectedly pulled my rather large body into his and gave me a big hug making me look small. He said, "How is that for a teddy bear hug?"

It took more courage for this man to open up and get help for his problems than it took for him to live in such a violent world with a violent lifestyle. After all, the life he was living was his norm and sharing what was deep inside was more threatening to him than the streets.

In order to overcome our fears and problems, I learned that we must face them. I like to use metaphors, analogies and case scenarios to keep it simple. The next two examples are related to something that I learned the hard way and that is, in order to overcome your problems, you must face them. That sounds simple and obvious, right? Maybe not.

Look at the many different things we do to avoid problems. There are drugs and alcohol use, acting like they don't exist, procrastinating, isolating, deflecting, blaming others, denying that the problem/s even exists and countless more. Here are some things that I say to my clients to keep it simple.

The first relates to *doing the dishes*. I have always hated doing the dishes. When I was no longer on a fixed income and began working, my goal was to save money to own a dishwasher. To me, I would be a success, and life would genuinely be good when I no longer had to do the dishes. Not only did I hate doing dishes, but I hated dealing with my problems.

Metaphorically speaking, the dishes are the problems. When I lived alone and because I hated doing the dishes, I would wait until they stacked up and I had no more clean ones to eat with before I chose to wash them. So, my kitchen was not clean, and by the time I decided to do the dishes, it would take an hour or more to do them.

On the other hand, I knew someone that had a system for doing the dishes. While eating, she was soaking what was used to cook the food, and as soon as we were done eating, she would wash what was in the sink and then soak the dishes we all ate from while socializing and listening to music. Fifteen minutes later, she would wash the dishes and utensils we ate with and her kitchen was always clean, and she was only using about fifteen to twenty minutes of work.

I tell clients do their "dishes" or in other words, face their problems when they occur and their "kitchen" or in other words, their life won't become unkempt, overwhelming and far more difficult to clean up than it needs to be.

In this other example, I explain that every neighborhood has a bully right? I then ask the client what happens when someone keeps running and running from the bully and usually the answer is that they continue to be chased and/or beat up.

I then ask what usually happens when that person stands up to the bully and faces him/her? The client usually says something like, they leave them alone or stops picking on them. I then ask them to look at their problems as the bully! I explain that if they keep running from their problems, their problems will keep chasing them. So, face your problems, stand up to them and deal with them, and they are more likely to go away.

In each of these examples, I often get this look as if a light came on in their head, followed by a smile. The client then says one of my favorite things and that is, "I never thought of it like that" or something like, "That's a pretty cool way of looking at it".

When it comes down to it, real men, real tough guys are those that pay their bills, are present with family and protect and provide. They are those that pay their child support, face their problems, do things when they don't feel like it (go to the doctor, AA/NA meeting, clean the house), and don't do things when they do feel like doing it (using drugs, being unfaithful or stealing).

Here are a couple more:

Here are a couple of quick ones that I use for those that are still using drugs or committing crimes: Do the right thing and you can't go wrong! Do the wrong thing and you can't go right! Play in dirt (unhealthy lifestyle) and you will get dirty (bad consequences). You cannot be successful down here when you are living up there in the clouds (being high or drunk). You must come down here with the rest of us to compete.

For me, doing the metaphoric dishes and overcoming adversity takes three important factors: Resilience, Courage and Faith. This is how I see it.

Thanks eHarmony

Thanks to the late Mr. E H. that made it even possible to be part of eHarmony. The website was in its infancy at the time, and I had only heard of it occasionally on TV commercials. It was something I had never even considered until Mr. H. suggested that I go through this dating site and try to find a soulmate, a girlfriend or maybe even a wife someday.

He suggested it after I told him that though I was working and had a nice apartment, it still wasn't a big deal to me because I did not have anyone to share my new life with. If anyone else had suggested eHarmony it would have gone in one ear and out the other. But it was E. H. This man had proven more than thirty years earlier at Bradley

Home, and countless times since, that he had my best interests at heart, so I gave it a try.

The first date I'll call a warm-up date. It was a nice dinner and some jazz music, but there was no chemistry. The second date was with Kim. We met for a very long date on January 21, 2006. I say a long date because it did not end until lunch and dinner had been eaten and digested. We talked for many, many hours nonstop and into the night. We wanted to get to know each other and talked about everything under the sun. We were comfortable with one another from the first words exchanged, and it only got better from there.

By the time our first date was over, we were high on life. I was enjoying my time with her more so than any drug or alcohol I had ever ingested. I found out, firsthand, what being high on life really meant. We continued to date, and things got better and better. I knew I had met someone special. I knew this because she kept asking more and more about me and my life. I was concerned at the beginning because whenever I have shared even a fraction of my history with women, they were gone, and I was left choking on the dust they left behind.

Unlike them, Kim told me that it had the opposite effect on her. She said the more she heard, the more she admired me and the more she wanted to know. I told her that this was very unusual, and she must be a special lady. I explained that I was a recovering alcoholic but had eight years clean and sober, at that time. I told her that if she wanted to have a drink to feel free because I did not expect to change her lifestyle when we had just met. She declined and said that she would never do anything to jeopardize my sobriety.

She promised at that moment, that if we ever got married, the night before the wedding would be the last drink she ever had for that reason. She has kept that promise. It was a little scary telling her to feel free to have a drink early on in our dating, but I did not want to scare her off. Any concerns I had ended quickly.

Seven weeks after we met, Kim was having a birthday. My mother had a trinket box for me to give to Kim for her birthday. I put the engagement ring inside of it. She opened the trinket box and saw the diamond ring. I asked the big question, she said yes, and the rest is history.

Four months later, we had signed the closing papers on our house, and three months after that, we were being married in front of the fireplace in the living room of our new home. Did you ever hear the expression God has a sense of humor? I ask this because a second-generation local magistrate was the man that married us. God's sense of humor was because back in my drinking days, I had faced charges in front of the first-generation magistrate, his father, and now his son was marrying me and my bride. Can you imagine that?

I have been truly blessed to have a wonderful woman in my life. This is the most important relationship, and one that takes work, compromise, good communication, thoughtfulness, selflessness and maybe most importantly, humor.

Anyone that knows Kim and me might think that we were followed around for a year before airing the Mike and Molly show. She and I have a very similar relationship to the characters on that show. Like Molly, Kim is very independent and is not afraid to say what is on her mind. Quite frankly, I need a strong woman to put me in my place if need be. She helps me to stay on course and lets me know when I begin to go off course.

She has a heart of gold and has been with me all the way, through the many medical problems I have had since we got married, most of which stemmed from my clumsiness, falls and subsequent injuries and surgeries.

Since we tied the knot, I broke my neck in a fall and had to have a cervical fusion. I fell and broke seven ribs in ten places, followed by pneumonia and sepsis. In my earlier years, I could always depend on my mother to be there. Today, I can depend on my loving and caring wife to be there. She takes great care of me as I have worked to get my strength and health back every time.

First and foremost, our marriage has worked because it's one that was meant to be. The other reason is that many relationships have one person that is a little stronger than the other financially, emotionally or in some other way. The other feels a need to stay for fear that they cannot make it without their partner. With Kim and me, we both have a good education (she too has a Master's Degree), good jobs and most importantly, lived on our own for decades before getting married.

She knows that if I kick her to the curb she would survive. I know that if she kicks me to the curb, I would survive. We are together because we want to be together not because one has leverage or power over the other. This, too, is why we operate as a team and not one calling the shots or controlling the other.

I feel like a teenager on his first date when I am with Kim. I love you and thank you for being a great support in my life. Thank you for being my sounding board as I became author of my first book.

Thank you, eHarmony, for connecting me with the love of my life.

Courage

To me, courage is facing challenges and fears unconditionally. That means that it doesn't matter what the situation is or what the odds are. It's continuing to move forward even when in doubt. It's also about sacrificing or jeopardizing your safety for a cause.

To me, courage requires adversity. It is the key factor. Without adversity, courage would not be needed. Faith is believing without proof. Resilience is bouncing back. So, when things are going well for you, it doesn't take much to "keep the faith" or to be resilient and "bounce back."

However, during times of adversity, courage is paramount. It's the critical piece. It is like unconditional love. Many can have faith, be faithful and keep bouncing back every day when life is good. Many begin to lose faith and have difficulty bouncing back when times get tough.

I say that courage is like unconditional love because it shows up when times are bad. Courage is your flashlight when life is dark and unsafe. People with courage rise to the occasion. Courage is looking adversity in the eye and saying, I will get through this. Courage is not giving up and bouncing back when you have been knocked down, only to get up the next day to confront your fears and your problems again and again. Courage gives you the will to have faith and be resilient when things look hopeless.

Courage is standing up for someone who is being bullied. Courage is continuing to move forward and keep trying, even when you don't feel like it because things look hopeless. Courage is not giving in to peer pressure when doing so would be the easier thing to do.

I did not realize it at the time, but courage has enabled me to have the rich and full life I have today. It has helped me get through many years of adversity. Courage is like my late mother's unconditional love. I remember her saying, "You will get through this and you will be a stronger and better person because of it." Thank God for blessing me with my mom and her words of wisdom and encouragement.

Courage is trying to achieve something when the evidence shows that the odds are slim to none.

Courage can be needed to do something as simple as just getting out of bed every day when you would rather be dead. I have clinical depression and became suicidal at nine years of age. How could I get out of bed when I felt hopeless, helpless and would rather have been dead? Depression has followed me all my life, and I still have periodic episodes of depression. But I have learned to live with it. I have learned that if I have the courage to keep getting out of bed and do things even when I don't feel like it, things will get better.

By the time I reached my teen years, my thoughts were so deranged that I thought that taking my whole bottle of pills and drinking a fifth of liquor took courage. I came to find that it takes far more courage to get up every day and put my best foot forward and just let things happen.

Courage has enabled me to get through total darkness so that I can see the light. All the adversity that I survived have been building blocks and stepping-stones to living a meaningful life. If I was "successful" with any of my many suicide attempts, I would not be here today. That also means that I would not have had the opportunity to change, grow and prosper.

I wouldn't have learned what I am truly capable of. I wouldn't know that I am in fact, "college material". You see, that used to be my response when people told me that I should go to college. My response would be laughter followed by the statement, "I am not college material".

Once I earned my college degrees, it was time to enter the workforce, a place that I knew little about. Because of my many different diagnoses and the problems that come with them, I was on welfare or

Supplemental Security Income (SSI) my entire adult life before earning my Bachelor's Degree. It was then, that the government determined that I was no longer disabled. Subsequently, I got a loan and eighteen months later, I had earned my Master's Degree.

Now it was time for fear set in again!!! Each time I reached a milestone and thought about getting to the next level, fear and doubt set in. This time was even a little scarier because to that point, I had an income. Although income was limited, it is something I will always be grateful to the state and federal government. For many years, it paid for my rent, all my medicines, medical bills and mental health treatment.

Now I would have the opportunity to *earn a living* as people say. At this chapter in my life, I had been seizure-free for 6-12 months and had been clean and sober for about 18 months. My thoughts swarmed me like bees from a beehive. All the "what ifs" stung me time and time again. What if my seizures return and I can't work anymore? What if I relapse with alcohol because I can't handle the pressure of the job? What if I become seriously depressed again or even become suicidal? I can't be a therapist or an effective worker if I am depressed and suicidal!

It took courage to look past all the realistic possibilities and tell myself that I certainly did not go to school all these years and owe all this money so I can sit at home and feel hopeless and useless. I was still thinking like a disabled person. I told myself "No!!!" You have spent all this time and the government's money to give yourself a fair chance to be a productive citizen in society. Moving forward would be a way to give thanks to God for helping you through everything. I'm thankful to the state of Pennsylvania and the federal government for the wealth of money provided to me while on a fixed income, and the thousands of dollars of government loans to pay for my college education. I shook the fears off and decided it was time to be a new and productive person in society.

I could do this by utilizing what I learned in school, along with my personal experiences, to help others. I was beginning to see that taking the risk was well worth it. I can now be a tax paying citizen so that my tax money can be used for those who are in need as I once was.

That is how I got the courage to decide to forget about the "what ifs" and use my Master of Social Work Degree to get a job and help others.

Because I had the courage to move forward, I have been a tax paying citizen for the last 20 years. I am free of seizures and alcohol since the late 1990s and have learned to live with my depression, PTSD and ADHD.

This once sad and lonely person is today a happily married man who drives a new car, is a homeowner and works full time as an Addiction Specialist.

I have worked in the field of mental health as well. I have taught classes at the community college. I have been a guest speaker at the University of Pittsburgh where I earned my Bachelor's and Master's Degrees in the field of Social Work. I am a motivational speaker as well. My wife and I were foster parents for a brief period, and I have been a big brother for the Big Brothers and Big Sisters of Western Pennsylvania.

Whether it was my learning disability, my seizures or the many other challenges I faced, my mother would encourage me by saying, "Don't give up, you will get through this and be a stronger and better person because of it". Many have told me how courageous it is for me to have not only made it through all my challenges, but exceeded the expectations

I think that I'm just stubborn but there might not be much of a difference between that and courage, and does it really matter?

Resilience

Resilience has been defined as bouncing back, showing elasticity during times of change or challenge. It also refers to being able to heal from trauma. Does anyone remember the plastic or rubber figures that were blown up and had the face of characters painted on them? They had weight in the base. As kids we used to punch and kick them. They would fall over, only to bounce right back up and rock back and forth until it stood upright again. It returned to the upright position, only to be punched and kicked again and again.

I threw more than a few blows at that thing. I was amazed at how hard I could hit it, and time after time it would bounce back. Every time it bounced back, I became more and more aggressive and more and more tired. It bounced back no matter what I did.

Early on I would find that amusing and impressive. By the fifth or sixth time I hit it or kicked it, I started to become short winded. I'd give one more swift punch, and then walk away. After I did, I would look back only to see it rebound and be standing straight up, and of course the face would be looking right at me. I could almost hear it say, "Go ahead! Try it again. You can't keep me down, with a little giggle under its breath".

That toy is symbolic of the abuse that my mind and body has endured based on how much I drank and for how long. A human being's physical and psychological capacity to tolerate and bounce back day after day is amazing.

Then I think about the other things that come with being a drunk. I have mentioned my seizure disorder and how many falls and injuries suffered from that, but then I think about the countless times I fell on my face, scraped my knees and the stitches required. All the scars and chronic pain are here to remind me every day of my nightmare relationship with alcohol.

Now add the countless fights. In the boxing ring, winning 65%-70% of the fights will lead to an early retirement and brain damage. But on the street, when you are up against baseball bats, knives and other paraphernalia, winning seven out of every ten times isn't bad, but I should have retired a lot earlier. Anything less than an undefeated record on the streets can get you killed.

When I was living that life and in the middle of that nightmare, it was just plain stupid. That is the cool thing about recovery. Stupid and self-destructive behaviors are transformed to or seen as resilience.

I believe that the evil forces (AKA Satan) are now frustrated because I kept bouncing back again and again. I have come to find that though Satan is still alive and well, he, like other abusers and negative forces, will have less and less influence on our lives. We become stronger, healthier and able to resist those temptations and challenging experiences he keeps putting in front of us.

I was taught that for every action there is an equal and opposite reaction. To me, the equal and opposite reaction to Satan is God. Unlike many, this is not a negotiable or debatable issue for me. If someone is atheist or agnostic, I respect your belief. I have heard that God does not need me to defend him, so I won't. I just think that He can be the only explanation for how I have managed to stay alive, bounce back and have a successful and happy life.

Faith

Faith has several different definitions, but the one I think about and refer to is "Believing without proof". This, too, can mean a lot of different things. Faith can also be related to religion like, "I'm of the Catholic or Jewish faith." If you'd like to, you can combine the two and Show faith by believing that there is a God despite not being able to physically see him (without physical proof).

I tried so hard to have faith but fell short more times than I can count. Like many, my faith began when I was a young child based on the values, traditions and beliefs of my parents and many others in the community at that time. I was brought up believing that there was a God, and that he provided blessings and watched over and protected us.

Faith was a double-edged sword for me because on one side, things were so bad in my life that I was desperate and had to believe that something better had to be ahead, and there certainly was no proof of that. On the other hand, those same terrible conditions of my earlier life made it very difficult to believe that there was a God. If there is, how could he allow all the terrible things that were happening in my life to continue? Where were the miracles that I heard could happen because that's what it would take to change the life that I was living?

I have come to find that things must take their course. Life is an ongoing process, and change is inevitable. I have also learned that faith is taking risks and without them there can be no gain. Let's just use my learning disability, ADHD, for an example. Though I passed my classes to move from one grade to the next, I constantly struggled. I certainly did not excel as I have in sports. My reading skills were poor because I had trouble with concentration and comprehension.

To get back to the definition of faith "Believing without proof." The "without proof" was certainly there but the believing part was not. If I didn't see proof in the time frame I wanted, the belief that it would happen wasn't there.

That is not an example of faith. That is an example of my need for immediate gratification or for getting the results I want within the time frame that I want them. This is what makes drugs and alcohol so attractive and desirable to many.

Faith is realizing that God had a plan for me all the way back when I was struggling to read. Today, I believe that he is with me as I write this book in hopes that it will help others who are struggling in school or in life due to a disability, an addiction or some other daunting problem. Faith is believing that in His time (not ours) you will not only get through it but exceed expectations.

EPILOGUE

My countless challenges had created physical and emotional pain that made me desperate for relief. I found relief in all the wrong places with drugs and alcohol. I had convinced myself that the physical pain could be numbed, if I drank enough. My emotional pain would be extinguished when I stopped caring and drank more.

I have learned through age and experience that I hurt because I cared. I also learned that if I really cared and was that desperate, it's more sensible to change my circumstances and my life rather than continue down the road I was on.

I had serious problems from early on but in retrospect, I made what was bad, far worse with the way I responded. Because I had been victimized so many times over so many years, I viewed myself as a victim. That became my identity. It was like putting glasses on and seeing the world through the lens of a victim. When I did this, I made choices from that perspective.

The shift from hopeless and helpless began to change when I chose to attend college. My choices were then made through a hopeful lens. This made me more optimistic, and it was self-empowering. My perspective changed, and I began to view things differently.

By taking the healthy risk to attend school, I found out what I am truly capable of and was quite surprised. Hope and positive change began when I refused to see life through the lens of a victim anymore. I found that just as negative things can progressively worsen, positive things can get progressively better. I chose to change my lifestyle and shift my energy. I began to invest my time in things that I have the power to change, while accepting the cards I have been dealt. In doing so things became simpler and easier.

My life has been like a magic trick in slow motion. I remember a magician showing me what his "magic" really consisted of, and I was surprised and felt foolish. What he was doing was simplistic and even dumb but deceptive and sneaky. This made the magic trick a cool thing. Life is like that too, if you keep it simple and go with the flow. I hope that some "tricks of the trade" are reflective of that.

Take it slow and do things with thought and care. Structure and routine are key for me because it minimizes the confusion and chaos. Choose healthy over unhealthy risks. Choose to associate with law-abiding and productive people who will enhance and support the life you want to live. Please know that there is no happy outcome when choosing to go down the path of addiction. The results are prison or worse.

I still struggle with problems like anyone else. Unlike the old days, however, I have mastered some skills that enable me to cope and contain my problems rather than making them worse. Pain and suffering are a reality, and I choose to face reality and confront my problems rather than running and avoiding them.

My energy is used to resolve my problems and to help others resolve theirs. My mission in writing this book is to educate, inspire, empower and instill hope for anyone and everyone who reads it.

I hope and pray that I have been able to do that. I love the view from where I am today because my world is bigger, brighter, clearer and happier.

Made in the USA
Middletown, DE
08 May 2021